The Wheel of Death

*the text of this book is printed
on 100% recycled paper*

THE
WHEEL
OF
DEATH

*A Collection of Writings from
Zen Buddhist and Other Sources
on*
DEATH—REBIRTH—DYING

Edited by PHILIP KAPLEAU
Assisted by PATERSON SIMONS

HARPER COLOPHON BOOKS
Harper & Row, Publishers
New York, Evanston, San Francisco, London

A hardcover edition of this book is available from
Harper & Row, Publishers

First HARPER COLOPHON edition published 1974

STANDARD BOOK NUMBER: 06-090377-5

FOR PERMISSION TO USE COPYRIGHTED AND NONCOPYRIGHTED MATERIAL GRATEFUL ACKNOWLEDGMENT IS MADE TO THE FOLLOWING:

GEORGE ALLEN & UNWIN, LTD. for extract from *Chuang-tzu* translated by Herbert Giles, copyright © 1889, 1926, 1961 by George Allen & Unwin, Ltd.; and R. D. M. Shaw for extracts from *The Embossed Tea Kettle and Other Stories* translated by R. D. M. Shaw, copyright © 1963 by George Allen & Unwin, Ltd.

EDWARD ARNOLD & CO. for extract from *Hinduism and Buddhism, Vol. I* by Sir Charles Eliot, copyright © 1921 by Edward Arnold & Co.

JOHN BLOFELD and RIDER & CO. for extract from *The Zen Teaching of Huang Po* translated by John Blofeld, copyright © 1958 by John Blofeld, published by Rider & Co.

BUDDHIST PUBLICATION SOCIETY and NYANAPONIKA MAHATHERA for extract from "Rebirth and the Western Thinker" (*Light of the Dhamma, Vol. V, No. 2,* April 1958) by Francis Story.

BRUNO CASSIRER (PUBLISHERS) LTD. for extract from *Buddhist Texts Through the Ages,* edited by Edward Conze.

DOUGLAS BURNS, M.D., for extract from his article, "Questions and Criticism of Buddhism" (*Suchness,* October 1968).

DOUBLEDAY & CO., INC. and LUCIEN STRYK for extracts from *Zen: Poems, Prayers, Sermons, Anecdotes, Interviews* by Lucien Stryk and Takashi Ikemoto, copyright © 1963, 1965 by Lucien Stryk and Takashi Ikemoto.

HARPER & ROW, PUBLISHERS, INC. for extracts from *Buddha and the Gospel of Buddhism* by Ananda K. Coomaraswamy, originally published by G. P. Putnam's Sons, 1916.

HOKUSEIDO PRESS for extracts from *Zen and Zen Classics, Vol. II* by R. H. Blyth, copyright © 1964 by R. H. Blyth; extracts from *Zen and Zen Classics, Vol. V* by R. H. Blyth, copyright © 1962 by R. H. Blyth; extract from *Zen in English Literature and Oriental Classics* by R. H. Blyth, published by Hokuseido Press, 1942.

PHILIP KAPLEAU for extract from a lecture by him; extract from *Tannisho: A Tract Deploring Heresies of Faith* translated by Philip Kapleau and A. Kondo, Higashi Honganji, Japan, 1961.

NĀRADA MAHĀTHERA for extracts from his article, "The Buddhist Doctrine of Kamma and Rebirth" (*Light of the Dhamma, Vol. III, Nos. 1 and 2*, June 1955 and January 1956).

OXFORD UNIVERSITY PRESS and LAMA GOVINDA for extract from the "Introduction" by Lama Govinda to *The Tibetan Book of the Dead* by W. Y. Evans-Wentz, published by the Oxford University Press.

PENGUIN BOOKS, INC. for extract from *Buddhist Scriptures* by Edward Conze, copyright © 1959 by Edward Conze.

RAMAKRISHNA-VIVEKANANDA CENTER and SWAMI NIKHILANANDA for extract from *The Gospel of Sri Ramakrishna* translated by Swami Nikhilananda, copyright 1942 by Swami Nikhilananda; extract from *The Yogas and Other Works* by Swami Vivekananda, copyright 1953 by Swami Nikhilananda.

SRI RAMANASRAMAM and T. N. VENKATARAMAN for extracts from *Talks with Sri Ramana Maharshi*, copyright © 1963 by Sri Ramanasramam; extracts from *Reflections on the Talks with Sri Ramana Maharshi* by S. S. Cohen, published 1959; extract from *The Teachings of Ramana Maharshi* edited by Arthur Osborne, copyright © 1962 by Sri Ramanasramam.

RANDOM HOUSE, INC. for extract from *The Stoic and Epicurean Philosophers* edited by Whitney J. Oates, copyright © 1940 by Random House, Inc.

RIDER & CO. and BHIKSHU SANGHARAKSHITA for extract from *The Three Jewels* by Bhikshu Sangharakshita, copyright © 1967 by Bhikshu Sangharakshita; and JOHN BLOFELD for extract from *The Wheel of Life* by John Blofeld, copyright © 1959 by Rider & Co.; extracts from *Ramana Maharshi and the Path of Self-Knowledge* by Arthur Osborne, copyright © 1963 by Rider & Co.; and LAMA GOVINDA for extracts from *Foundations of Tibetan Mysticism* by Lama Govinda, copyright © in the English translation 1959 by Rider & Co.

ROUTLEDGE & KEGAN PAUL, LTD. for extract from *The Lankavatara Sutra* translated by Daisetz Teitaro Suzuki, copyright © 1932 by Routledge & Kegan Paul, Ltd.

JOHN WEATHERHILL, INC. for extracts from *The Three Pillars of Zen* by Philip Kapleau, copyright © 1965 by Philip Kapleau.

RŌSHI YASUTANI for extracts adapted from his booklet *Eight Bases of Belief in Buddhism* translated by Tai Eido Shimano.

Even as night darkens the green earth
the wheel turns, death follows birth.
Strive as you sleep with every breath
that you may wake past day, past death.

CONTENTS

PERSONAL ACKNOWLEDGMENTS

The debt of gratitude which the editor owes the distinguished contributors to *The Wheel of Death* will be obvious to all who read these pages. With hands palm to palm he gratefully salutes the Buddha and the Zen masters, Chuang-tzu and Lao-tzu; Socrates and Voltaire; Ramana Maharshi and Ramakrishna; Rōshi Yasutani, Lama Govinda, Nārada Mahāthera, and Bhikshu Sangharakshita; John Blofeld, Francis Story, and Dr. Douglas Burns; and translators Swami Nikhilananda, Ven. Shimano, R.H. Blyth, Lucien Stryk, R.D.M. Shaw, and Edward Conze.

His deep thanks also go to Paterson Simons, editor of the newsletter *Zen Bow* (where much of this material first appeared), who worked closely with him on every aspect of the book from researching, selecting, and editing the material to writing portions of the Introduction.

Audrey Fernandez, a charter member of the Zen Center of Rochester, New York, contributed considerable time and skill in making the English adaptation of the Heart of Perfect Wisdom (Prajnā Pāramitā), for which he is deeply appreciative. The editor is also indebted to her for the English rendering of the Epigraph (chanted nightly in Zen monasteries), as well as for numerous suggestions which greatly improved the quality of the text.

Special thanks are due Martin and Alice Provensen, designers of the dust jacket and symbols inside the book, for their personal interest and cooperation.

The editor is most grateful to deLancey Kapleau, his wife, for her comments and unstinting help in the writing of the article on "Practical Instructions to the Dying." Her long training in Zen made her an especially valuable collaborator.

Karen Feibusch of Harper & Row has been an understanding and helpful editor, and he would like to express his appreciation of her efforts.

Finally, his sincere thanks to Marce Wilcove for her conscientious and intelligent attention to every detail of the typing and proofreading of the manuscript.

A NOTE ON THE DRAWINGS

Wheel: one of the principal symbols of Buddhism. When eight-spoked it is the Wheel of the Dharma "turned" by the Buddha—that is, the eternal Law as taught by him. It is also emblematic of the Eightfold Noble Path leading to enlightenment. The six-spoked wheel is the "Wheel of Life and Death," corresponding to the six realms of unenlightened existence (q.v.).

Skull rosary: The skull, which survives the disintegration of the flesh and sinews, symbolizes both the impermanence of the body and the indestructibility of Buddha-nature.

Endless knot: stands for the infinite network of interrelationships between all forms of life.

Phoenix: a mythical bird of great beauty which lived for five hundred years in the desert. It immolated itself on a funeral pyre and then rose from its own ashes in the freshness of youth, living another cycle of years; represents death and regeneration.

Flame passing from lamp to candle: indicates that rebirth is the continuation of a process rather than the transfer of a substance.

Circle: symbolic of the oneness, or indivisibility, of all life. Nothing can be added to or subtracted from a circle; in the same way, man's true nature is whole and complete.

INTRODUCTION

This little volume grew out of a series of articles on "Death, Rebirth, and Dying" which first appeared in *Zen Bow*, the publication of the Zen Center of Rochester, New York; it is largely composed of selections from the writings of ancient and contemporary seminal minds in both East and West. The series was inspired by a mounting concern in America with the perfunctory treatment of the dying and the widespread attitude of disguising or ignoring the fact of death. Although much has been written about the psychological, sociological, and physical aspects of death, curiously, little has been said about the vital need for spiritual guidance through the dying process and the Intermediate stage, as it is known, that follows death.

Long ago the *Egyptian Book of the Dead*, and later the *Tibetan Book of the Dead*, provided such practical instructions. But these ancient texts have the disadvantage of presenting data couched in terms often too esoteric for modern Americans. The "Practical Instructions to the Dying" in this book do not attempt to furnish the same kind of detailed information as the older writings provided, yet they are a guide to the dying which can in their own way accomplish what the Egyptian and Tibetan books of the dead accomplished in theirs. These instructions are really a call to Life, a call to the living no less than the dying to awaken to the true significance of birth and death.

A viable art of dying in our own day could go a long way toward relieving the dehumanized atmosphere of the average hospital death, which has become a tragic sign of our times. Inherently medical practice expresses deep compassion, but that compassion seems to have gone increasingly astray as the art and religion of death have become drowned in the science of prolonging life at any cost. "To die in a hospital, probably while under the mind-benumbing influence of some opiate, or else under the stimulation of some drug injected into the body to enable the dying to cling to life as long as possible," says Evans-Wentz in his preface to *The Tibetan Book of the Dead*, "cannot but be productive of an undesirable death, as undesirable as that of a shell-shocked soldier on a battlefield. Even as the normal result of the birth-process may be aborted by malpractices, so similarly may the normal result of the death-process be aborted."

In fairness to the medical profession, however, it can be said that the practice of thwarting the death-process through infusions and injections reflects a cultural pattern which not only sees all pain as pointless but which looks upon death as the "last great enemy," to be outwitted and subdued at all costs. Death, which ought to be welcomed as natural and inevitable, becomes the Grim Reaper and dying the terror of all terrors. Yet studies have shown that when the mental state of dying patients is not disturbed by sedation or other medication—in other words, when they are fully conscious and capable of responding to their environment with awareness unimpaired—their predominant emotion is not fear but calmness, the more so if they have established belief in the rebirth-process.[1]

Many in the West, convinced of the validity of the doctrine of rebirth, have searched among Buddhist and other Asian teachings for further knowledge of the revolving phases of life and death. Unlike the linear theology of the West, Buddhism teaches that life and death present the same cyclic continuity observed in all aspects of nature. It says that the life and death of animate matter is, in each instance, merely the seen aspect of an unending stream of cause and effect which, though appearing to emerge from and sink into the earth at two points, nonetheless has an unseen subterranean existence and appears at other places in other times and in other shapes.

The assertion that nothing precedes birth or follows death is largely taken for granted in the West, but however widely believed, it is still absurd from a Buddhist viewpoint. Such an assertion rests on the blind assumption—in its own way an act of faith—that life, of all things in the universe, operates in a vacuum. It asks us to believe that this one phenomenon, the invigoration of supposedly inert matter, springs out of nowhere and just as miraculously disappears without a trace. Most people who hold such views consider themselves "rational," and yet in this question of life and death they deny the conservation of energy, one of the essential laws of physics.

Men who have seen life and death as just such an unbroken continuum, the swinging of an eternal pendulum, have been able to move as freely into death as they walked through life. Socrates went to the grave almost perplexed by his companions' tears. Many of the Zen masters actually anticipated their "final" hour, meeting it with equilibrium and even laughter, sometimes sitting in the full lotus posture or, more rarely, standing on their heads. In fact, the Zen masters were so intimately involved with the *whole* of existence that they found overinvolvement with any of its parts, death included, to be a misplaced concern, saying to people who asked about an afterlife, "Why do you want to know what will happen to you after you die? Find out who you are now!"

To some this last may seem at variance with the Buddhist doctrine of rebirth. On closer examination, however, such statements by the masters actually complement this teaching. The masters more than anyone else are aware that Self-realization dissolves the *problem* of rebirth by revealing that birth and death are present in every moment, that rebirth sits on the bed of death even as death beckons rebirth. In responding in this fashion, therefore, they are simply impressing upon the questioner the need to realize his true nature, and to divert him from merely a speculative concern with the future.

The selections from Zen Master Hakuin in the "Rebirth" section, vividly describing the Buddhist hells and habitual modes of behavior—i.e., karmic patterns—by which human beings *comdemn themselves* to such states, may likewise seem incongruous to some. Yet it must be remembered that Hakuin was a deeply enlightened, highly accomplished Zen master with remarkable powers. What he writes therefore cannot be dismissed as the quaint hellfire-and-damnation fantasies of a "fundamentalist" oriental mind.

No meaningful discussion of rebirth is possible, moreover, without an understanding of karma, the law of action, reaction, and interaction that lies at the heart of both Buddhism and Hinduism. For this reason, writings on this vital subject have been included in the section preceding "Rebirth."

A word about the order of the material in *The Wheel of Death*. Logically, the natural time sequence would seem to be dying, death, and rebirth. But since the average person comes to the experience of death with little understanding of it and therefore with considerable trepidation, the selections on death and rebirth are presented first in the hope of allaying his fears.

The sacred texts and selections in this anthology can, if carefully studied and practiced, help the dying person achieve a calm and deliberate death, facilitate a satisfactory rebirth, and even liberate him from painful bondage to birth and death. And they can hearten the living by making them realize that death after all, like life, is also transitory.

One: **DEATH**

DEATH

Birth is not a beginning;
death is not an end.

—Chuang-tzu

Death is the protest of the spirit
against the unwillingness of the formed
to accept transformation—the protest
against stagnation.

—Govinda

Unlike life, death cannot be taken
away from man, and therefore we may
consider it as *the* gift of God.

—Seneca

Lama Govinda:

It may be argued that nobody can talk about death with authority who has not died, and since nobody apparently has ever returned from death, how can anybody know what death is or what happens after it?

The Tibetan will answer: "There is not *one* person, indeed not *one* living being, that has *not* returned from death. In fact, we all have died many deaths before we came into this incarnation. And what we call birth is merely the reverse side of death, like one of the two sides of a coin, or like a door which we call 'entrance' from outside and 'exit' from inside a room."

It is much more astonishing that not everybody remembers his or her previous death, and because of this lack of remembering, most persons do not believe there was a previous death. But likewise they do not remember their recent birth, and yet they do not doubt that they were recently born. They forget that active memory is only a small part of our normal consciousness, and that our subconscious memory registers and preserves every past impression and experience which our waking mind fails to recall.

There are those who, in virtue of concentration and other yogic practices, are able to bring the subconscious into the realm of discriminative consciousness and thereby to draw upon the unrestricted treasury of subconscious memory, wherein are stored the records not only of our past lives but the records of the past of our race, the past of humanity and of all pre-human forms of life, if not of the very consciousness that makes life possible in this universe.

Socrates:
To fear death, gentlemen, is nothing other than to think oneself wise when one is not; for it is to think one knows what one does not know. No man knows whether death may not even turn out to be the greatest of blessings for a human being; and yet people fear it as if they knew for certain that it is the greatest of evils.

Apollonius of Tyana:
There is no death of any one but only in appearance, even as there is no birth of any save only in seeming. The change from being to becoming seems to be birth, and the change from becoming to being seems to be death; but in reality no one is ever born, nor does one ever die.

Epictetus:
And what is the end of the illness? Nothing worse than death. Will you realize once for all that it is not death that is the source of all man's evils, and of a mean and cowardly spirit, but rather the fear of death? Against this fear then I would have you discipline yourself; to this let all your reasonings, your lectures, and your trainings be directed; and then you will know that only so do men achieve their freedom.

Sri Ramana Maharshi:
Owing to the I-am-the-body notion, death is feared as being the loss of Oneself. Birth and death pertain to the body only, but they are superimposed on the Self, giving rise to the delusion that birth and death relate to the Self.

Why do you mourn the loss of your parents? I shall tell you where they are: they are only within ourselves and are ourselves. For the life-current has passed through innumerable incarnations, births and deaths, pleasures and pains, etc., just as the water current in a river flows over rocks, pits, sands, elevations and depressions on its way, but still the current is unaffected. Again, the pleasures and pains, births and deaths are like undulations on the surface of seeming water in the mirage of the ego. The only reality is the Self from where the ego appears, and runs through thoughts which manifest themselves as the universe and in which the mothers and fathers, friends and relatives appear and disappear. They are nothing but manifestations of the Self.

The Buddha:

Disciples, there is a realm in which there is neither earth nor water, fire nor air; not endless space, infinite consciousness, nor nothingness; not perceptions nor nonperceptions. In it there is neither this world nor another, neither sun nor moon. I call it neither a coming nor a going nor a standing still; not death, nor birth; it is without basis, change, or stability. Disciples, it is the end of sorrow.

For that which clings to another there is retrogression, but where there is no clinging there is no retrogression. Where no retrogression exists calm exists, and where there is calm there is no obsessive desire. Where obsessive desire is absent, there is neither coming nor going, and where coming and going have ended there is no death, no birth; where death and birth do not exist there is neither this life nor an afterlife, nor any in between—it is, disciples, the end of suffering.

Yet there is an Unoriginated, Unborn, Uncreated, Unformed. If this Unoriginated, Unborn, Uncreated, Unformed did not exist, there would be no liberation for whatever is originated, born, created, and formed. But since there is an Unoriginated,

Unborn, Uncreated, Unformed, liberation is possible for whatever is originated, born, created, and formed.

Rōshi Yasutani:

What we see [in the world] is illusory, without substance, like the antics of puppets in a film. Are you afraid of dying? You need not be. For whether you are killed or die naturally, death has no more substantiality than the movements of these puppets. Or to put it another way, it is no more real than the cutting of air with a knife or the bursting of bubbles, which reappear no matter how often they are broken.

Having once perceived the world of Buddha-nature, we are indifferent to death, since we know we will be reborn through affinity with a father and a mother. We are reborn when our karmic relations impel us to be reborn. We die when our karmic relations decree that we die. And we are killed when our karmic relations lead us to be killed. We are the manifestation of our karmic relations at any given moment, and upon their modification we change accordingly. What we call life is no more than a procession of transformations.

If we do not change, we are lifeless. We grow and age because we are alive. The evidence of our having lived is the fact that we die. We die because we are alive. Living means birth and death. Creation and destruction signify life.

When you truly understand this fundamental principle, you will not be anxious about your life or your death. You will then attain a steadfast mind and be happy in your daily life. Even though heaven and earth were turned upside down, you would have no fear. And if an atomic or hydrogen bomb were exploded, you would not quake in terror. So long as you became one with the bomb what would there be to fear? "Impossible!" you say. But whether you wanted to or not you would perforce become one with it, would you not? . . . .

Master Keizan:
   To see the body is to see the mind, to know the mind is to grasp the body: they are identical. Appearing, they do not add a jot; disappearing, not a particle is lost. The four combined elements created your body, while the destruction of all phenomena results in the mind. To understand the Way and realize the mind, one does not have to seek far.

Master Dōgen:
   It is fallacious to think that you simply move from birth to death. Birth from the Buddhist point of view is a temporary point between the preceding and the succeeding, hence it can be called birthlessness. The same holds for death and deathlessness. In life there is nothing more than life, in death nothing more than death: we are being born and are dying at every moment.
   Now as to conduct: In life identify yourself with life, at death with death. Abstain from yielding and craving. Life and death constitute the very being of Buddha. Thus should you reject life and death you will be the loser, and yet you can expect no more if you cling to either. You must neither loathe, then, nor covet, neither think nor speak of these things. Forgetting body and mind by placing them together in Buddha's hands and letting him lead you on, you will without design or effort gain freedom, attain Buddhahood. . . .

Master Hakuin:
   And again, it is extremely foolish to think that one must wait till after one's death in expectation of obtaining all these benefits [of zazen meditation]. It is also the most culpable negligence. Do not grieve as though this is all a matter of something in the far distance. If it was a matter of having to see or hear

something in China or India, far beyond the seven-fold tides of the seas, one might grieve. But what we are trying to do is to look at our own mind with our own mind—and that is something closer to us than looking at the pupils of our eyes with our eyes. And do not grieve as if it were something very deep that we are trying to look at. If it were a matter of something to be seen or listened to at the bottom of the nine-fold chasm or under the thousand fathomed depths of the sea, we might grieve—but to look at my own mind with my own mind is less [i.e., more easily done] than smelling my own nose with my own nostrils!

Master Shōzan (Shao-shan)

A man said to the master, "Of course I never think of death."

To which the master responded, "That's all very well, but you'll not get very far in Zen, I'm afraid. As for myself, well, I train in Zen in detestation of death and in hope of deathlessness, and I am resolved to carry on in this way from life to life until I realize my aim. That you do not think of death shows that you are not a man of enlightenment, because you are incapable of knowing your Self, whatever there is in you that uses the six sense organs."

Master Dōgo (Tao-wu)

The Master Dōgo once took a disciple with him when he went to console a grieving family. When they arrived, the disciple, named Zengen, knocked on the coffin lid and asked Dōgo, "Is he alive or dead?"

The master replied, "I won't say he's alive, I won't say he's dead."

Zengen exclaimed, "Why won't you tell me one way or the other?"

Dōgo answered, "I won't say. I won't say."

On their way back to the temple Zengen said, "I warn you, Master, if you won't tell me, I'll knock you down!"

Dōgo answered, "Do whatever you want! But you won't get a word out of me." So Zengen hit him.

Long after, when Dōgo himself was dead, Zengen visited Sekisō (another of Dōgo's disciples) and told him about the incident. Then Zengen asked, "Was he alive or was he dead?"

Sekisō answered, "I won't say he was alive, I won't say he was dead."

Zengen asked, "Why won't you tell me?"

Sekisō said, "I won't say! I won't say!"

Zengen suddenly came to a profound insight.

Teitoku Matsunaga:

> The morning glory blooms but an hour
> > and yet it differs not at heart
> from the giant pine
> > that lives for a thousand years.

Master Ikkyū:

> > Born like a dream
> In this dream of a world,
> > How easy in mind I am,
> I who will fade away
> Like the morning dew.

> One prays for the life of tomorrow,
> > Ephemeral life though it be.
> This is the habit of mind
> > That passed away yesterday.

> The Buddha-nature
> > Means non-birth, non-extinction.
> Then know that illusion
> > Is birth, death, rebirth.

Lao-tzu:
Death arises from life itself.
For every three out of ten born
Three out of ten die.
But why in the face of death
Should any three out of ten go on breeding,
When all they produce is more death?
Because of the wild obsession to multiply.
But there is only one out of ten, so they say, so sure of life
That the tiger and the wild bull avoid him in the hills
And weapons turn from him on the field of war.
The wild bull cannot find a place in him to pitch its horn,
The tiger cannot find a place in which to dig its claws,
The weapon's point can find no place in him to pierce.
And why?
Because when he dies he does not die.

Chuang-tzu
After the death of Chuang-tzu's wife, Hui-tzu visited the master to express his condolences. He arrived to find Chuang-tzu sitting on the ground, with his legs spread wide apart. The widower was singing away and whacking out the tune on the back of a wooden bowl.

"You lived all these years with your loving wife and watched your eldest boy grow to manhood. For you not to shed a tear over her remains," exclaimed Hui-tzu, "would have been bad enough. But singing and drumming away on a bowl—this is just too much!"

"Not so," the master replied. "I am a normal man and grieved when she was dead. But then I remembered that she had existed before this birth. At that time she was without a body. Eventually, substance was added to that spirit and, taking form, was born. It is clear to me that the same process of change which brought my wife to birth eventually brought her to death, in a way as natural as the progression of the seasons. Winter follows autumn. Summer follows spring. To wail and groan while my wife is sleeping peacefully in eternity would be to deny these natural laws of which I cannot claim ignorance. So I refrain."

"All that has form, sound and color may be classed under the head *thing*. Man differs so much from the rest and stands at the head of all things simply because the latter are but what they appear and nothing more. But man can attain to formlessness and vanquish death. And with that which is in possession of the eternal how can mere things compare? . . . .

"A drunken man who falls out of a cart, though he may suffer, does not die. His bones are the same as other people's, but he meets his accident in a different way. His spirit is in a condition of security. He is not conscious of riding in the cart, neither is he conscious of falling out of it. Ideas of life, death, fear, etc., cannot penetrate his breast and so he does not suffer from contact with objective existences. And if such security is to be got from wine, how much more is it to be got from Tao [the Way]. It is in Tao that the sage seeks his refuge, and so he is free from harm."

"Lao-tzu was born when it was time for him to be born and no sooner. He also died when the natural process of life had expired in him. Paeans of joy at his birth or wailing at his death would be vulgar and show us to be ignorant of the order of Nature. In ancient days a sage who had transcended birth and death was said to have cut the Thread of Life. People fear death only because they fail to see that life and death are not separate states but merely two stages of one natural process—that both are present in any given moment. Just as flames mark the burning of wood, so life is the energy released in the aging and death of the body. Even though the wood is reduced to ashes, the energy released as fire radiates throughout eternity, and though men come and go the flame of life burns eternally."

Two: KARMA

KARMA

If you want to know the past [cause],
look at your present life [effect]. If you want
to know the future [effect], look at your
present [cause].

—The Buddha

We are the heirs of our actions.

—The Buddha

We ourselves are responsible for our
own happiness and misery. We create our
own heavens. We create our own hells. We
are the architects of our fate.

—Nārada Mahāthera

Swami Vivekananda:

Karma in its effect on character is the most tremendous power that man has to deal with. Man is, as it were, a centre and is attracting all the powers of the universe towards himself, and in this centre is fusing them all and again sending them off in a big current. Such a centre is the real man, the almighty and the omniscient. He draws the whole universe towards him; good and bad, misery and happiness, all are running towards him and clinging round him. And out of them he fashions the mighty stream of tendency called character and throws it outwards. As he has the power of drawing in anything, so has he the power of throwing it out.

All the actions that we see in the world, all the movements in human society, all the works that we have around us, are simply the display of thought, the manifestation of the will of man. . . . This will is caused by character, and character is manufactured from karma. As is the karma, so is the manifestation of the will. The men of mighty will the world has produced have all been tremendous workers—gigantic souls with wills powerful enough to overturn worlds, wills they got by persistent work through ages and ages. Such a gigantic will as that of a Buddha or a Jesus could not be obtained in one life, for we know who their fathers were. It is not known that their fathers ever spoke a word for the good of mankind. . . . The gigantic will which manifested Buddha and Jesus—whence did it come? Whence came this accumulation of power? It must have been there through ages and ages, continually growing bigger and bigger until it burst on society as Buddha or Jesus, and it is

19

rolling down even to the present day.... Our karma determines what we deserve and what we can assimilate. We are responsible for what we are; and whatever we wish ourselves to be we have the power to make ourselves. If what we are now has been the result of our own past actions, it certainly follows that whatever we wish to be in the future can be produced by our present actions. So we have to know how to act....

Nārada Mahāthera:

Kamma (karma in Sanskrit) literally means action or doing. Any kind of intentional action whether mental, verbal or physical is regarded as kamma. It covers all that is included in the phrase "thought, word and deed." Generally speaking, all good and bad actions constitute kamma. In its ultimate sense kamma means all moral and immoral volition. Involuntary, unintentional or unconscious actions, though technically deeds, do not constitute kamma, because volition, the most important factor in determining kamma, is absent....

Kamma does not necessarily mean past actions. It embraces both past and present deeds. Hence, in one sense, we are the result of what we were; we will be the result of what we are. In another sense, it should be added, we are not totally the result of what we were; we will not absolutely be the result of what we are. The present is no doubt the offspring of the past and is the parent of the future, but the present is not always a true index of either the past or the future; so complex is the working of kamma. For instance, a criminal today may be a saint tomorrow; a good person yesterday may be a vicious one today.

Lama Govinda:

In Buddhist parlance, karma loses its power and is dissolved in the light of perfect knowledge. As long as karma remains the force of the dark and impenetrable past, it is of fixed and unalterable magnitude, which we feel as "the power of fate," against which we struggle in vain. In the moment of profound intuition or enlightenment, the past is transformed into a *present* experience, in which all the moving forces and circumstances, all inner and outer connections, motives, situations, causes and effects—in short the whole dependent origination, the very structure of reality—are clearly perceived. In this moment the Enlightened One becomes master of the law, the master-artist, in whom the rigid necessity of law is transformed and dissolved into the supreme freedom of harmony.

Master Shinran

. . . Master Shinran told me [his disciple]: "Evils as insignificant as even a speck of dust on the tip of a rabbit's hair or a sheep's fleece are brought about by karmic law—this you should know." On another occasion he asked me: "Do you believe everything I tell you?"

"Yes, Master," I answered.

Again he asked: "Well, now, are you sure you won't disobey me?"

"Yes, I am sure," I answered respectfully.

Whereupon he said: "Will you murder a thousand men?[2] If so, I definitely assure you of rebirth in the Pure Land."

To this I answered: "I respect what you say, but I am incapable of murdering even a single man."

Master Shinran continued: "Then, why did you say you would not disobey what I, Shinran, told you? . . . . Now, you see, if you had free will you would have no compunction about murdering even a thousand men upon being told that by so doing you could attain rebirth [in the Pure Land]. But because there is no karmic necessity for you to kill even a single person, you do not commit murder. That is why you do not kill, not because you are good. On the other hand, even though you did not want to kill, you might nevertheless kill hundreds or thousands of people."

Questions of King Milinda to the Venerable Nāgasena

"Venerable Nāgasena," asked the king, "why are men not alike, some short-lived and some long, some sick, others healthy, some ugly and some handsome, some weak and some powerful? Why are certain men poor and others rich, why some base and others noble, some stupid and some clever?"

The Elder replied, "Your Majesty, why are plants not alike, some astringent, some salty, some pungent, some sour and some sweet?"

"I suppose, Venerable Sir, because they come from different sorts of seeds."

"That is how it is with men, your Majesty! They are not alike because their karmas are not alike. As Buddha said, 'Each being has its own karma. Each is born through karma, becomes a member of a tribe or family through karma. Each is subject to karma—it is karma that separates the high from the low.' "

"Very good, your Reverence!"

Francis Story:

Buddhism teaches that one of the most important, if not *the* most important, functions of the mind is that of *willing*. Under this aspect the mind is called *cetanā*, which denotes its capacity for willed intention. And cetanā, the Buddha declared, is kamma (volitional action). The will to act is followed by the action; action in its turn is followed by result. Thought is therefore a creative act. It was from this that Schopenhauer derived the central theme of his *Die Welt als Wille und Vorstellung,* which makes will the dominating factor in the universe. The creative act of thought may be good or bad, but whichever it may be, it can only produce results of a like nature to the causes it originates. The moral principle of the universe is a scientific law. . . .

Rōshi Yasutani:

. . . The law of causation means that an effect inevitably follows a cause. In mathematics if we add two and two, the invariable result is four. The same is true when we subtract three from ten and are left with seven. . . . Regardless of time or place or the persons involved, the ups and downs of human life are also determined by this law. . . . When we actually face our own personal happiness or unhappiness, however, we tend to ignore cause and effect, saying, "This is an accident" or "This is my fate" or "This is divine will," and the like. Those who speak this way do not understand the relationship between cause and effect, which includes past, present, and future. . . .

There are many aspects to this law of causation. . . . One involves a minor cause and a major effect. Here time is a factor, for the longer the lapse of time between the cause and the effect the greater the effect. For example, if you save money, the longer you keep it in a bank the greater the amount of interest you receive. On the other hand, if you have a debt—financial or moral—and do not repay it over a long period, it becomes larger by reason of the added interest. . . . Think of your good deeds as savings and your bad deeds as debts.

Now, we also must consider the relationship of individual to collective karma. Even as each of us has an independent existence, at the same time we relate deeply to one another; thus it is not always easy to distinguish between collective and individual karma. Actually karma in its working is very subtle and complex. Suppose I neglect my health and become sick. This is individual karma and no one can substitute for me in this illness; I alone have to take the medicine. However, collective karma would begin to operate if I became seriously ill, perhaps needing an operation, so that my family and friends became concerned about me. My family's finances would be affected too. To be a passenger in a plane or a car that crashes—this is also collective karma. But that one passenger dies, another is only injured, and still another escapes unharmed—this is individual karma. . . .

Now let me explain fixed and variable karma. Our fixed karma is the result of previous actions crystallized at the time of birth and unchangeable until death. For example, to be born as a man or woman is fixed karma, a condition we cannot alter. To be born white or black or Japanese or Chinese is likewise unchangeable.

Variable karma is karma which can be changed by one's own effort. Consider the matter of health. A person may be born sickly, but by watching his health can become strong. Similarly, a healthy person who neglects himself can become weak. Longevity is a matter of both fixed and variable karma, fixed because limited by our genetic inheritance, variable because it is also affected by one's honesty and good will. A kind and honest person is more apt to extend his life [because of his composure], whereas an irascible and dishonest one very likely will shorten it [by creating anger and tension in himself and others].

When the law of causation is misunderstood it can be made to sound like fatalism. The notion of fatalism arises only if one believes the relation between cause and effect is fixed. Cause and effect, however, are dynamic, the effect always changing according to the circumstance. Take two farmers who plant seeds of grain at the same time. One cultivates his field, fertilizing it with rich manure, the other does nothing but watch the weeds. Will there not be a great difference in their respective crops? . . . .

Regardless of the effect, there is always a primary and a secondary or contributing cause. Consider a bean plant. Seeds are the primary cause of its existence, but to grow, these seeds require soil, water, and sunlight. Had the bean seeds been kept in their dried condition they would not have sprouted, flowered, nor produced new beans no matter how many years elapsed. What was required were secondary causes, in this case soil, water, and the light of the sun.

In the same way, when we pass from this life to the Intermediate state at "death," though impelled by our desire to be born again as a human being, we cannot do so without parents, who are a necessary contributing cause for birth.

There is one more aspect of the law of causation which needs to be set forth and that is the relation between an effect and one's acceptance of it. We sometimes have a tendency to think that effects are irreversible since they result from primary and secondary causes. Nevertheless, depending upon our attitude, a bad effect may be turned to a good end. Suppose one is sentenced to jail. This is an effect of a previous action. How one chooses to accept the situation, however, is up to him. He may have a change of heart and become law-abiding or, as an old offender, tell himself to be more careful and not get caught the next time. On the other hand, he may make his jail his spiritual training center by practicing zazen and reading good books. Obviously his attitude toward his confinement will greatly alter its effect upon him.

Fatalism, then, is a misconception of the Buddhist law of causation. Nothing is fixed. . . . Man and his environment are not separate and apart. One's situation is not ordered by either gods or devils but is a natural consequence of one's own actions. We express ourselves by thought, speech, and action even though we are unaware of the meaning of good and bad. These actions echo within us and influence our personality. When our attitudes change, our circumstances likewise change. . . .

Philip Kapleau:

The workings of karma are complex and often unfathomable. A son is suddenly killed in an accident, and in their anguish and despair the parents protest, "Why did this have to happen to *our* child? He was such a generous, loving person with no malice in him. Why did *he* have to die so young and so violently when others whose lives are selfish and cruel die in their own bed at a great age? Where is the justice of it?" And if previously they had faith in the goodness of God, they now feel disillusionment and bitterness toward Him. "Why would a loving and just God permit this?" they demand. . . .

A person who accepted karma (i.e., the law of causation on the moral plane) would never be impelled to ask such questions. When tragedy struck him the question would not be "Why?" but "How?"—"How can I rid myself of the 'bad' karma which brought this about and create 'good' karma in the future which will benefit myself and others?" One who truly understood that whatever we reap was once sown by us would inevitably say, "I don't know why this has happened, but since it has I must have deserved it." Regardless of the time, place, or nature of it, death —one's own or someone else's—would be seen as the inevitable consequence of a concatenation of causes and effects. One therefore would not be impelled to try to understand what on the surface appeared to be a meaningless death.

My own teachers used to say, "No matter how painful a particular event of your life and how seemingly inscrutable and remote its cause, if you put your palms together in gratitude for the opportunity it offers to repay a karmic debt, your pain will be lightened and your karmic burden lessened. Furthermore, there will be no residue of resentment or bitterness."

Such an attitude is not unknown in the West. In Europe in ancient days there were peoples who used to teach their children when they burned a finger, for instance, to thank the fire immediately and not curse it.

The Sixth Patriarch of Zen said, "When others are wrong I am in the wrong. When I have done wrong I alone am to blame." Such a deep sense of personal responsibility could come only from one who truly understood the law of causation, who knew that the network of interrelationships between all forms of life is so vast and complex that we cannot disavow responsibility for whatever happens anywhere, least of all for the repercussions on other lives of our *own* thoughts and actions.

One of the leaders of a new religion in Japan, Tenko-San, relates an incident which is germane here. Observing a young mother slapping her small son he asked, "Why did you slap him?"

"My boy just slapped another child," she replied.

"But the wrong done is the same in both cases, isn't it?" said Tenko-San.

"Is there a better way than to slap a child in such a case?" the mother asked.

"Yes, I think there is. You might have frankly acknowledged your son's wrongdoing by bowing down to the other child, saying, 'Please slap me on the head for having taught my child to conduct himself in such a wrong manner.' "[3]

The ordinary person's reaction to a painful situation is quite different. He is quick to blame his wife or his parents or his friends or his boss or society or fate or God—almost anything but himself—for his sufferings. . . .

The acceptance of the doctrine of karma and rebirth has far-reaching implications. No child who had been reared to believe in the validity of the law of causation could one day fling into the face of his parents the taunt, "Don't blame me! I didn't ask to be born!" for he would know that we all ask to be born and are born through parents with whom we have a karmic affinity. He would be aware that the primary cause of our being propelled again and again into rebirth is a clinging to the notion of a separate, individual existence and a craving for the enjoyments of the senses, and that the secondary, or contributing, cause is a mother and a father. No child who understood the depth of the parent-child karmic relationship could ever permanently alienate himself from his parents, for he would understand that the consequences, spiritually speaking, would be disastrous. Nor could parents with similar awareness of the law of karma ever exclaim in exasperation, "We just don't understand how any child of *ours* could do such a thing!" since they would realize that their sons and daughters have a karma—i.e., "habit forces" or tendencies of long standing—which is independent of inherited mental and physical characteristics. Children would not become bitter toward their parents for acts of commission or omission; they would accept their parents' shortcomings as the inevitable burden of unexpiated karma. Children thus would not feel driven to renounce their parents, nor would fathers and mothers feel impelled to run the lives of their children. Parents would recognize that they cannot blame their

children for the pains of parenthood, while children would realize that the domineering attitudes of their parents are the prod-
uct of causes and conditions which they (the children) once set
in motion. Both would know that mutual respect and love in the
parent-child relationship, as in every other, grows from pain as
much as from joy. . . .

If we took the law of cause and effect seriously, we would
think twice before recklessly lying, cheating, maiming, and de-
stroying, because we would know that sooner or later the day
of reckoning will come both in our individual lives and collec-
tively as a nation. . . .

There is yet another aspect to the law of causation. Our hori-
zons would expand and our lives take on fresh meaning if we
began training ourselves to see that even the minutest event in
our lives has karmic significance. We would gain a new awareness of our own power and dignity even as we would become
more humble, for we would realize that we are not isolated
fragments thrown into the universe by a capricious fate, but one
vast ocean in which all currents intermingle. . . . Wonder and
joy would replace boredom and frustration.

Rōshi Yasutani:

Let me tell you a well-known Zen kōan which will help explain the law of causation more fully. This kōan is found in the
book of kōans known as *Mumonkan,* or *The Gateless Gate.* It
is titled "Hyakujō's Fox." Hyakujō is the Japanese name for
Hui-hai, a famous Zen master of the T'ang era.

Whenever Hyakujō delivered a sermon a certain old man was
always there listening to it together with the monks; when they
left the hall he left also. One day, however, he remained behind
and Hyakujō said to him, "Who may you be?"

The old man replied, "I am not a human being. In the far

distant past I was the head monk here. On one occasion a certain monk asked me whether an enlightened man was subject to the law of cause and effect, and I wrongly answered that he was not. Thus for five hundred lives I have been reborn as a fox. I now beg you to release me from this animal rebirth by causing a change of mind through your words." Then he asked Hyakujō, "Is an enlightened man subject to the law of causation or not?"

Hyakujō answered, "No one can set aside the law of cause and effect."

The old man immediately awakened and making his bows said, "I am now released from rebirth as a fox; my body will be found on the other side of this mountain. I wish to make a request of you. Please bury me as a dead monk."

Hyakujō had one of the head monks sound the wooden clappers and inform the monks that after the midday meal there would be a funeral service for a dead monk. The monks thought this odd, as all were in good health, nobody was in the infirmary, and they wondered what the reason could be for this order. After they had eaten, Hyakujō led them to the foot of a rock on the farther side of the mountain, and with his staff poked out the dead body of a fox and had it cremated.

In the evening Hyakujō ascended the rostrum in the lecture hall and told the monks, "If you preach at random out of your halfway satori, you will suffer the pangs of hell. I don't know whether you noticed, but whenever I gave my daily lectures a fox disguised as an old man attended them. Long ago he had been head monk at this monastery. Once he had stated that with perfect enlightenment one is no longer subject to the law of cause and effect, and because of this half-truth he became a fox for five hundred rebirths. He has now repented his error and from the bottom of his heart asked me for the truth. I told him, 'Even all the Buddhas of the Three Worlds can't cheat the law of causation.' With that he came to sudden and complete enlightenment, being released from the life of a fox. Since he asked to be buried as a monk, we have done so. You must all be careful how you teach others."

Whereupon Hyakujō's senior monk, Ōbaku, rose, bowed down to his teacher three times and loudly stated, "Because of your correct answer that old man was released from the life of a fox. But suppose he had never made a mistake. How would he have fared? A fox becomes a man, a man a heavenly being, a heavenly being a Bodhisattva, a Bodhisattva a Buddha, and after a Buddha what? At last there is no place to go. Give me an answer!"

Hyakujō replied, "Just come closer and I'll tell you the answer."

Ōbaku, understanding what his teacher had in mind, went up to him—and boxed his ears. Hyakujō, clapping his hands and laughing, exclaimed, "I was intending to slap you but instead was slapped myself."

My own teacher, Rōshi Harada, said that Hyakujō's Fox is a very important kōan, illustrating the fact that a cause is always accompanied by an effect. Zen Master Dōgen also emphasized its importance in his famous book, *Shōbōgenzō*, stating that although this kōan may be misunderstood the law of causality can never be cheated.

Mumon, the author of the *Mumonkan*, has this verse at the conclusion of the kōan:

> Subject to or not subject to
> Are two faces but one die.
> Not subject to or subject to—
> Wrong, all wrong.

The fox here implies the power of our real nature—in other words, the power of the universe. The principles of Buddhism are an explanation of this power, and Zen practice is grasping this dynamic power and taking it into our life and personality. If you grasp the fact that "subjection to the law of causation and freedom from it" are one, it's truly simple. But if you analyze them, they become separate and false, and no matter how hard you reason about it a trace of contradiction always remains.

Every existence is a momentary form appearing according to prevailing conditions, without a fixed form of its own. This absence of a fixed form is freedom from the law of causation; having a form which accords with the conditions of the moment is subjection to the law of causation. Therefore the very subjection to the law of causation is tantamount to our freedom from it.

A moving picture, as you know, appears according to the conditions of the film, light, and screen—the picture itself has no specific form of its own. Having no form of its own, it changes according to the movement of the film. This can be called subjection to the law of causation. At the same time having no form of its own is its freedom, or "emptiness" aspect. So—Mumon says—

> For the truly enlightened man
> Subjection to the law of cause and effect
> And freedom from it
> Are one truth.

Tibetan Master Milarepa:

Thoughtful persons, once having heard about the doctrine of karma and believing in it will be able to put forth similar zeal and energy [to mine]. But those who hear the words and have not realized their significance will be unable to break attachments to wordly life. Therefore it is of greatest importance to develop faith in the doctrine of karma. Some people seem unable to grasp the karmic significance of even the simplest events. They devote themselves to various explanations of the void as taught in the sutras, not realizing that the doctrine of the void is far more subtle and intricate than the doctrine of karma, more difficult to comprehend and more difficult to believe in. But once one has actually grasped the doctrine of the void, its very essence includes that of the law of karma. A man who has grasped the void thus necessarily acquires more subtle powers of judgment, and his capacity for distinguishing good from evil grows more refined. In short, he becomes much more conscientious. . . .

If one does not believe firmly in the law of karma, one will inevitably lack zeal in the pursuit of his devotional practices. But if one does believe firmly in the law of karma, the thought of miseries in the Three Lower States is sure to fill one with dread and inspire one with the intensest desire for Buddhahood. Then one's faith and humility as regards the Guru, zeal and energy in meditation [zazen], and finally the way one bears the experiences of spiritual growth will equal mine in every way. . . .

So I exhort you all to establish a firm belief in the law of karma. Meditate upon, consider, and weigh deeply the biographies of other saints, the law of karma, the discomforts and miseries of all *samsāric* existence, the difficulties of acquiring a well-endowed human body, the certainty of death, and the uncertainty of the exact time of death. Ponder these things and then devote yourselves to study and practice. . . .

The Buddha:

If it is true that a man *must* reap according to his deeds, in that case there is no religious life, nor is any opportunity afforded for the complete extinction of suffering. But if the reward a man reaps *accords* with his deeds, in that case there is a religious life and opportunity is afforded for the complete extinction of suffering. . . .

And what kind of individual would it be whose pain-producing actions, however slight, bring him to a hellish state? Whenever an individual is not proficient in the management of his body, is not proficient in the precepts, is not proficient in concentration, is not proficient in wisdom, is limited and bounded and abides in what is finite and evil: that is the sort of individual whose pain-producing actions, however slight, would bring him to a hellish state.

Said the Buddha: The ignorant cling to names, ideas, and signs; their minds move along these channels. As thus they move along, they feed on multiplicities of objects and fall into the notion of an ego-soul and what belongs to it, and cling to appearances. As thus they cling, there is a reversion to ignorance, and they become tainted; karma born of greed, anger, and folly is accumulated. As karma is accumulated again and again, their minds become swathed in the cocoon of discrimination as the silk-worm; and, transmigrating in the ocean of birth-and-death, they are unable, like the water-drawing wheel, to move forward. And because of folly they do not understand that all things are like *māyā*, a mirage, the moon in water, and have no self-substance to be imagined as an ego-soul and its belongings; that things rise from their false discrimination; that they are devoid of qualified and qualifying, and have nothing to do with the course of birth, abiding, and destruction; that they are born of the discrimination of what is only seen of the Mind itself; and assert that they are born of . . . time, atoms, or a supreme spirit, for they follow names and appearances. The ignorant move along with appearances.

Three: **REBIRTH**

REBIRTH

I died as mineral and became a plant,
I died as plant and rose to animal,
I died as animal and I was a man.
Why should I fear? When was I less
by dying?

                                        —Rumi

Why should not I come back as often as I am
capable of acquiring fresh knowledge, fresh
experience? Do I bring away so much from
one life that there is nothing to repay the
trouble of coming back?

                                        —Lessing

After all, it is no more surprising
to be born twice than it is to be born once.

                                        —Voltaire

Rōshi Yasutani:

In a work by the fifth-century Indian patriarch Vasubandhu our life is illustrated as a wave.[4] A wave arises when the energy of the wind passes through water, and that wave by its energy in turn produces the next wave. If there is no resistance or friction, the movement of the wave continues endlessly. This is seen from the law of the conservation of energy, according to which no energy is ever lost. Now, the same energy that created a particular human being will produce a new life in the same way that the energy of one wave produces the next. This energy force does not disappear but goes on to create a succession of lives. Another name for it is karma. Just as the waves on the face of the ocean are different, so each individual is unique. However, in the depths of our nature, in the ocean itself, all individual existences in heaven and earth are equal.

Were they asked about the movement of the water of a wave, most people would say it is horizontal, but actually it is vertical; the only thing that moves horizontally is the energy. Another mistaken notion about a wave is that it arises in a specific place and then disappears. Now, just as many people mistakenly think of a wave as the movement of one specific area of water, so many believe there is an unchanging substance called "I," and that this fixed "I" continues to exist from yesterday to today, from today to tomorrow. . . .

Were I to stand up and then move a few feet, it would generally be thought that the same person made both movements, but this is not so. The truth is that the person who got up and the one who moved forward are not one and the same. This can

41

be made clearer by comparison with a moving news bulletin. The letters are apparently moving, but as we know, each letter is in fact formed separately by the rapid flashing on and off of lights and there is no movement of the letters.

Many see the moment of what is called death as the termination of a particular life or consciousness; the energy which constituted that individual, they are convinced, is lost forever. . . . Buddhism, however, teaches that our life is created and destroyed from moment to moment and that a new self is continuously being formed.

In the book by Vasubandhu mentioned above our life is also compared to the "continuous sweep of a waterfall." A waterfall appears to be one great mass of water, but actually it is composed of an infinite number of droplets which are constantly changing according to their composition. The name "waterfall" is simply an arbitrary designation. What we take to be a continuous movement is really a series of fragmentations. So it is with our life: fragmentary moments within an endless continuum. What we call "myself" is not a fixed substance.

It is important to understand clearly the concept "birth and death." Buddhism teaches that there are two types of birth and death. One is ordinary birth and death, i.e., from the moment of our physical birth to the moment of our body's death; the other, momentary birth and death. Most people, unaware of this, think that one and the same person lives continuously from physical birth to death. To correct this misunderstanding let us use the motion picture as an illustration.

We know that the motions of an actor on a movie screen are determined by the movement of the film. Each frame of the film is similar to, yet slightly different from, the next. As the frames are viewed one after another this slight difference causes the actor on the screen to move. The frames change in such rapid succession that it seems as though one person were moving continuously.

Momentary birth and death is exactly like the unrolling of a film; it is a continuous process of creation and destruction. But because we cannot see the momentary changes we conclude it is the same person who continues to exist.

The continuity of life as described by Vasubandhu is shown below:

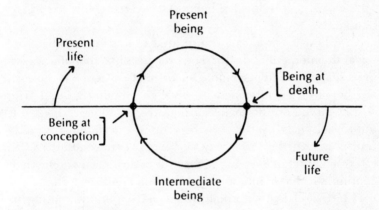

"Being at conception" refers to the moment of the union of sperm and ovum. We are born, become children, then move on to adulthood and old age. All this is our being in the present. What we experience when we die is our being at death. Needless to say, no one doubts his own existence at conception, during his present life, and at death; but many question a continuation of life beyond that. What, then, about the law of the conservation of energy, which asserts that no energy is ever lost? To claim that this tremendous force behind our human activities permanently disappears at the moment of death is like saying that one wave does not produce another.

Again according to Vasubandhu, at the moment of death our life energy is transmitted to an intermediate form of being, and this state, too, is subject to constant change, not unlike our present existence, which is void of a fixed core. . . .

This intermediate state of being is said to be superior to existence on a mundane level in that it has the power, like an electric current, to pass through all obstacles, even being capable of movement which covers hundreds of miles in a moment's time. Intellect, emotion, and will, but of a tenuous nature, are said to exist on this level of being. There are even sense organs of a kind. . . .

Now, how is our karma transmitted to this intermediate being at the moment of death? The process is like that of impressing a seal on muddy ground. Our present existence is the seal, our being on an intermediate level the muddy ground. The design carved on the seal is karma. At the moment the seal is impressed on the surface of the ground the design is exactly transposed; in the same way all karma is transmitted to this intermediate state of being at the time of death. This being then continues its life of momentary birth and death, as well as ordinary birth and death, normally in seven-day periods, waiting for the opportunity to be conceived.[5] This intermediate being is even said to have the mysterious power of seeing, feeling, and finding its parents-to-be, and to be aware of the sexual intercourse by which it may be conceived.

Nãrada Mahãthera:

For a being to be born here a being must die somewhere. The birth of a being—which strictly means the arising of the Aggregates, or psycho-physical phenomena, in the present life—corresponds to the death of a being in a past life; just as in conventional terms the rising of the sun in one place means the setting of the sun in another. This enigmatic statement may be better understood by imagining life as a wave and not as a straight line. Birth and death are only two phases of the same process. Birth precedes death, and death, on the other hand, precedes birth. This constant succession of birth and death in connection with each individual life-flux constitutes what is technically known as saṁsāra—recurrent wandering.

There also are some extraordinary persons, especially children, who, according to the laws of association, spontaneously develop the memory of their past births and remember fragments of their previous lives. A single such well-attested respectable case is in itself sufficient evidence for a discerning student to believe in a past birth. "Pythagoras is said to have distinctly remembered a shield in a Grecian temple as having been carried by him in a previous incarnation at the siege of Troy." Somehow or other these wonderful children lose that memory later, as is the case with many infant prodigies.

Douglas Burns, M.D.:

Rebirth is the continuation of a process rather than the transfer of a substance. If we light a match and with the match light a candle, the process of combustion in the match is carried over to the candle. Is the flame in the candle the same flame or a different one than the one in the match? We can say both yes it is or no it is not. Likewise the Buddha said that when one dies it is not quite correct to say that same person will live again, nor is it correct to say that he will not live again. The truth lies between these two extremes. Or again we can illustrate the problem in this way: A four year old child grows up to become a forty year old adult. Though by name it is the same person at either age, in essence the two are totally different personalities in both mind and body. What is it that persists from the four year old to the forty year old? Very little if anything. Or what is it that persists from the fertilized ovum in the mother's uterus to the child? The younger being is a process which interacts with the world around it to eventually evolve into the other. In similar manner when a person dies, the mental conditions set up by the terminating personality carry on, producing effects in a future personality.

Ananda Coomaraswamy:

Or, again, we could not offer a better illustration, if a modern instance be permitted, than that of a series of billiard balls in close contact: if another ball is rolled against the last stationary ball, the moving ball will stop dead and the foremost stationary ball will move on. Here precisely is Buddhist rebirth: the first moving ball does not pass over, it remains behind, it dies; but it is undeniably the *movement of that ball*, its momentum, its karma, and not any newly created movement, which is reborn in the foremost ball. Buddhist rebirth is the endless transmission of such an impulse through an endless series of forms; Buddhist salvation is the coming to understand that the forms, the billiard balls, are compound structures subject to decay, and that nothing is transmitted but an impulse, a *vis a tergo*, dependent on the heaping up of the past. It is a man's character, and not a self, that goes on. . . .

Questions of King Milinda to the Venerable Nāgasena

The king asked: "Venerable Nāgasena, is the person who is reborn the same person [who died], or a different person?"

"He is neither the same person nor is he different."

"Give me an illustration."

" . . . Suppose, your Majesty, a man were to light a lamp. Would that lamp burn all night?"

"Yes, Venerable Sir, it would."

"Well, your Majesty, is the flame that burns in the first watch of the night the same flame that burns in the second watch of the night?"

"No, Venerable Sir, it is not."

"Is the flame, your Majesty, that burns in the second watch the same that burns in the third watch?"

"Venerable Sir, it is not."

"Then, your Majesty, was the lamp in the first watch a different lamp in the middle watch and an even different one in the third?"

"No, Venerable Sir, the light comes from the same lamp all night long."

"In just this way, your Majesty, a human being is the uninterrupted succession of physical and mental states. As one state passes away another is born, and it occurs in such a way that there is no differentiation between the preceding and succeeding states. Therefore, it is neither the same person nor a different person that goes to the final summation of consciousness."

Francis Story:

Much misunderstanding of the Buddhist doctrine of rebirth has been caused in the West by the use of the words "reincarnation," "transmigration" and "soul."

. . . "Soul" is an ambiguous term that has never been clearly defined in Western religious thought; but it is generally taken to mean the sum total of an individual personality, an enduring ego-entity that exists more or less independently of the physical body and survives it after death. The "soul" is considered to be the personality-factor which distinguishes one individual from another, and is supposed to consist of the elements of consciousness, mind, character and all that goes to make up the psychic, immaterial side of a human being. . . .

The Buddha categorically denied the existence of a "soul" in the sense defined above. Buddhism recognizes the fact that all conditioned and compounded phenomena are impermanent, and this alone makes the existence of such a "soul" impossible. . . .

What then is the "identity" between a person in one life and the "same" person in another which justifies the use of the word "rebirth"? The answer is that it is purely a serial relationship—an "identity" of a certain kind which can only be described in terms of a causal continuum.

. . . Precisely how is human rebirth accomplished? The answer is that the thought-force is attracted to the physical conditions of human procreation which will enable it to re-manifest and thus give expression to its craving-potential. The released energy in some way operates on and through the combination of male and female generative cells on much the same principle as that of the electric current working on the filaments in the lamp to produce light. The blind creative power of the craving-potential then adapts and develops them, moulding the structure of their growth in such a way as to make it serve its purpose within the limitations it carries with it in its kamma. In this it is also restricted, of course, by the general characteristics of the racial group and other distinctive categories to which the parents belong, but even within this limiting frame-work there are still infinite variations of physical and mental characteristics to be developed by the influence of the past kamma. To infer that all Chinamen are alike, only because what is most noticeable to us is the manner in which they differ from ourselves, is as absurd as to say that all Englishmen or all Russians are alike.

Bhikshu Sangharakshita:

Buddhism teaches rebirth. Not, indeed, in the sense of an unchanging immaterial entity (*ātman*) transmigrating from one physical body to another, but in a deeper, subtler sense. Just as, in the present existence, a preceding becomes the condition for

for a succeeding mental state, so in dependence on the last thought-moment of one life arises the first thought-moment of the next, the relation between the two lives, as between the two mental states, being one of causal continuity. The illustration appropriate to the case is not that of a man who changes from one set of clothes to another, the man himself remaining the while unchanged, but rather that of a flame which, in its advance, feeds upon successive bundles of fuel. . . .

To say that, at death, the psychical life ceases with that of the body is one extreme view; to say that any psychical element, such as an immortal soul, survives death unchanged is the other. Here, as elsewhere, Buddhism follows the Middle Path, teaching that the "being" of one life is neither exactly the same as, nor completely different from, the "being" of another life. Though consenting to speak in terms of rebirth, it precludes misunderstanding by pointing out that there is no one who is reborn. . . .

Lama Govinda:

In practically every Tibetan temple a vivid pictorial representation of the six realms of the samsāric world can be found. And corresponding to the nature of this world, in which the endless cycle of rebirths takes place, the six realms are represented as a wheel whose six segments depict the six main types of worldly, i.e. unenlightened, existence. These forms of existence are conditioned by the illusion of separate selfhood, which craves for all that serves to satisfy or to maintain this "ego," and which despises and hates whatever opposes this craving.

These three basic motives or root-causes of unenlightened existence form the hub of the wheel of rebirths. . . .

[These qualities of] greed, hatred and delusion condition each other and are inseparably connected. They are the ultimate consequences of ignorance concerning the true nature of things, on account of which we regard transient things as permanent and unreal things as real and desirable. In mentally and spiritually undeveloped beings, governed by blind urges and subconscious drives, this lack of knowledge leads to confusion, hallucinations and delusion, which involves us more and more in the rounds of saṁsāra, the chasing after ephemeral happiness, the flight from suffering, the fear of losing what has been gained, the struggle for the possession of desirable things and the defense or protection of those that have been acquired. The saṁsāra is the world of eternal strife and dissension, of irreconcilable contrasts, of a duality which has lost its balance, due to which beings fall from one extreme into the other.

Conditions of heavenly joy are opposed by states of infernal tortures; the realm of titanic struggle and lust for power is opposed by the realm of animal fear and persecution; the human realm of creative activity and pride of accomplishment is opposed by the realm of "hungry spirits," in whom unsatisfied passions and unfulfilled desires lead a ghost-like existence. . . .

Devas [i.e., those in the realm of the gods] lead a carefree life, dedicated to aesthetic pleasures. . . . On account of this one-sided dedication to their own pleasures, they forget the true nature of life, the limitations of their existence, the sufferings of other beings as well as their own transiency. . . . They live, so to say, on the accumulated capital of past good deeds without adding any new values. They are gifted with beauty, longevity and freedom from pain, but just this lack of suffering, of obstacles and exertion, deprives the harmony of their existence of all creative impulses, all spiritual activity and the urge for deeper knowledge. Thus finally they sink again into lower states of existence. Rebirth in heavenly realms, therefore, is not an aim which Buddhists think worth striving for. It is only a temporary suspension, but no solution to the problem of life. It leads to a strengthening of the ego-illusion and to a deeper entanglement in the saṃsāric world.

... The reverse side of those heavenly pleasures [is] the realm of infernal pain. These infernal sufferings ... are not "punishments" that have been inflicted upon erring beings by an omnipotent god and creator but the inevitable reactions of their own deeds. The Judge of the Dead does not condemn but only holds up the mirror of conscience, in which every being pronounces his own judgment. This judgment, which seems to come from the mouth of the Judge of the Dead, is that inner voice ... [which is in reality] an emanation of Amitābha in the form of Avalokita who, moved by infinite compassion, descends into the deepest hells and—through the power of the Mirror of Knowledge (which arouses the voice of conscience)—transforms suffering into a cleansing fire, so that beings are purified and can rise to better forms of existence. ...

Master Hakuin

"I don't need to tell you that these are terribly important times. Sentient things are pressing each other on their journey back to what was their former home—the three hells. One can see them before one's very eyes being pushed down into those terrible places, the hells of weeping and wailing ... where they will have to undergo the pains of unmeasured suffering. ...

"The Tathāgata [i.e., the Buddha], who controls the ten powers of Buddhahood, resides entirely within the minds of all sentient beings who intrepidly aspire to Buddhahood.

"Unfortunately, other sentient beings, not so intrepid but negligent and indolent, must, as has been said, pass through the three stages to Nirvāna.

"What then? This immediate attainment of Buddhahood by the one realization is entirely the exertion of one moment of absolute energy.

"And who and what are the other sentient beings? They are beings, like you and me, who have attained to the stage of existing in a human body, which is so hard to come by in the course of the cycle of ages, and have looked upon the law of the Buddha, which again is so hard to discover or come by in that same course of ages. But they look upon this law as if they were in a dream. They feel as if they were going to live for a thousand years. They eat what they want to eat, they drink what they want to drink, they sleep when they want to sleep, they play when they want to play, and their perception of the Buddha wisdom is as small as a rape seed! . . . . Every day they commit the ten evils, the three sins of the body, the four sins of the mouth, and they pile them up to carry with them as they go on towards the land of darkness.

"When these people die, at first they do not have a proper body, and it is as if they had entered into a deep sleep. But after a little while their 'root-nature' becomes fixed, and then they open their eyes and find that they have fallen into the city of darkness. They begin to notice the mountain of 'After-Death' and the valley of the three hells. Then they have to grope their way for ten or twenty miles till they come out onto a broad, limitless plain, where there is no sun or moon but only great conflagrations burning with the flames flaring up to the sky. Here they see sinners crowded together weeping bitterly. And the new-comers think, 'Alas, have we sunk down to this dreadful place? Oh, if only we had known about this . . . but we thought all the talk about this sort of thing was the idle talk of men of false views. And nobody had ever come back to tell us about it, so we concluded that there was no such place. But in any case, we have not committed murder or any great crimes sufficient to drag us into these hells. . . .'

"Well, there is no end to what I might say about these hells. And, everybody, this is not a matter for other people to think about. It is our own affair."

"This mind, which all of us possess, is what is important. It must be kept firm and resolute. . . . It may bring forth a Buddha, or it may build up a hell. It is the most untrammelled and wicked fellow. So do not let anybody be careless about it. . . . If we could see some shape or form of our mind, riotous with the five lusts, reflected in some mirror for us, it would be a repulsive sight, from top to bottom. Men after long ages of rebirth at last come to birth in this world of men and then they behave like hungry demons, or like even lower grades of demons, and even like devils. They never stop striving for fame. From morn to eve, in high ranks and low ranks, there is the lust of property and the lust for sensual pleasures. The whole heart is clouded and the bright world becomes dark. Oh! so dark, dark, dark. . . . The original Amida and the Buddha who dwell in us are painted over with the impurities of the ten wickednesses and the eight falsities till at last they are so splashed and smarmed over that they cannot be recognized. And it is we ourselves, who with our own hands do this! We build up our own hells! What does this is the false or non-Buddha nature in us. . . .

"The non-Buddha nature shows itself in those who hold the false view which keeps a man attached to the idea that this body of ours is utterly brought to an end at its death and that this world, and with it this body, will continue to inexhaustible eternity. It is the nature which thinks itself smart and clever in its worldly wisdom. It is a state of spiritual laziness. It has no discernment of the law of Karma, and selfishly indulges in the three poisons and the five lusts. . . ."

A soldier named Nobushige came to Hakuin and asked, "Do heaven and hell really exist?"

"Who are you?" inquired the master.

"I am a samurai," the warrior replied.

"You, a samurai?" exclaimed Hakuin. "What kind of ruler would have you as his guard? You have the face of a beggar!"

Nobushige became so angry that he reached for his sword, but Hakuin continued on, "So you have a sword! Well, your weapon is still probably much too dull to cut off my head!"

As Nobushige drew his sword, Hakuin looked right at him and exclaimed, *"That* is hell!"

Sheathing his sword, the samurai bowed with great humility and respect.

"And *this,*" Hakuin announced, "is heaven."

John Blofeld:

What we call "life" is a single link in an infinitely long chain of "lives" and "deaths." Perhaps if our unconscious could be raised to conscious level we should be able to perceive the entire chain stretching back far enough to exceed the most generous estimates of the length of time human beings have populated this earth. (And why just this earth? Why should not many of our previous lives have been passed upon other earths contained within this stupendous universe?) Perhaps the recollection would include hundreds or thousands of millions of lives lived here or elsewhere, and at this or other levels of consciousness, perhaps in states of being previously unsuspected. Only it is hard to understand how any mind could encompass so vast an accumulation of memories.

We have no sure means of knowing the duration of the interval between each death and rebirth, but most Teachers have held that this present life leads us forwards or backwards from precisely the point reached by the end of the preceding life. (Thus the belief that a man may immediately be reborn as a pig or, conversely, as a god would seem to be a popular misunderstanding of the implications of the doctrine of reincarnation—an over-simplification of a little-understood truth.) Yet, though a person's ever-changing "individuality" is carried over from life to life in the form of karmic propensities, it is very sure that the newborn baby has to acquire all knowledge of the *objective* world afresh. For, if inherited karmic propensities included conscious memories, then babies would be born as wise as their grandparents. Childhood is chiefly spent in relearning the forgotten language of touch, sight, hearing, taste and smell, from which an entirely new set of deductions has to be drawn. On the other hand, abstract propensities, including talents, bents, abilities, personal likes and dislikes, and a host of others may perhaps remain intact throughout the journey across the borders of death and rebirth. It is the method of applying these propensities to the exterior world which has to be relearnt. . . .

The Buddha

"The senses are as though illusions and their objects as dreams. For instance, a sleeping man might dream that he had made love to a beautiful country girl, and he might remember her when he awoke. What do you think— . . . does the beautiful girl he dreamed of really exist?"

"No, Lord."

"And would the man be wise to remember the girl of his dreams, or to believe that he had really made love to her?"

"No, Lord, because she doesn't really exist at all. . . ."

"In just the same way a foolish and ignorant man of the world sees pleasant forms and believes in their existence. Hence he is pleased, and so he feels passion and acts accordingly. . . . But from the very beginning his actions are feeble, impeded, wasted, and changed in their course by circumstances. . . . And when he ends his days, as the time of death approaches, his vitality is obstructed with the exhaustion of his allotted span of years, the karma that fell to his lot dwindles, and hence his previous actions form the object of the last thought of his mind as it disappears. Then, just as the man on first waking from sleep thinks of the country girl about whom he dreamed, the first thought on rebirth arises from two causes—the last thought of the previous life as its governing principle, and the actions of the previous life as its basis. Thus a man is reborn in the purgatories, or as an animal, a spirit, a demon, a human being, or a god. . . . The stopping of the last thought is known as decease, the appearance of the first thought as rebirth. Nothing passes from life to life, but decease and rebirth take place nevertheless. . . . But the last thought, the actions (karma), and the first thought, when they arise come from nowhere and when they cease, go nowhere, for all are essentially defective, of themselves empty. . . . In the whole process no one acts and no one experiences the results of action, except by verbal convention."

Sri Ramana Maharshi

Q: Do intellect and emotions survive death?

A: Before considering that, first consider what happens in your sleep. Sleep is only the interval between two wakings. Do these survive in this interval? They represent the body-consciousness and nothing more. If you are the body, they always hold on to you. If you are not, then they do not affect you. The one who was in sleep is the one who is speaking now. You were not the body in sleep. Are you the body now? Find out this, and the whole problem will be solved.

Q: Should I not try to escape rebirth?

A: Yes. Find out who is born and who has the trouble of existence now. When you are asleep do you think of rebirths or even the present existence, etc.? So find out whence the present problem arises and there is the solution also.

"That which is born must die. Whose is the birth? Were you born? How do birth and death affect the eternal Self? Think to whom these questions occur and you will know."

Q: Do a person's actions in this life affect him in future births?

A: Are you born now? Why do you think of future births? The truth is that there is neither birth nor death. Let him who is born think of death and palliatives for it.

"See how a tree grows again when its branches are cut off. So long as the life source is not destroyed it will grow. Similarly, latent potentialities withdraw into the heart at death but do not perish. That is how beings are reborn.

"In truth, however, there is neither seed nor tree. . . ."

Sri Ramakrishna

Nanda: Is there no afterlife? What about punishment for our sins?

Master: Why not enjoy your mangoes? What need have you to calculate about the afterlife and what happens then, and things like that? Eat your mangoes. You need mangoes.

The Buddha

In a dialogue the Buddha replies to a wandering monk named Vaccha, who questioned him about the undetermined problems, and in answer to every solution suggested says that he does not hold that view. Vaccha asks what objection he has to these theories that he has not adopted any of them.

"Vaccha, the theory that the saint exists (or does not exist) after death is a jungle, a desert, a puppet show, a writhing, an entanglement, and brings with it sorrow, anger, wrangling and agony. It does not conduce to . . . the absence of passion, to the cessation of evil, to peace, to knowledge, to perfect enlightenment, to nirvāna. Perceiving this objection, I have not adopted any of these theories."

"Then has Gotama any theory of his own?"

"Vaccha, the Tathāgata has nothing to do with theories, but this is what he knows: the nature of form, how form arises, how form perishes: the nature of perception, how it arises and how it perishes (and the same with the other skandhas). Therefore I say that the Tathāgata is emancipated because he has completely and entirely abandoned all imaginations, agitations and false notions about an ego and anything pertaining to an ego."

"But," asks Vaccha, "when one who has attained this emancipation of mind dies, where is he reborn?"

"Vaccha, the word 'reborn' does not fit the case."

"Then, Gotama, he is not reborn?"

"To say he is not reborn does not fit the case, nor is it any better to say he is both reborn and not reborn, or that he is neither reborn nor not reborn."

"Really, Gotama, I am completely bewildered and my faith in you is gone."

"Never mind your bewilderment. This doctrine is profound and difficult. Suppose there was a fire in front of you. You would see it burning and know that its burning depended on fuel. And if it went out you would know that it had gone out. But if some one were to ask you, to which quarter has it gone, East, West, North or South, what would you say?"

"The expression does not fit the case, Gotama. For the fire depended on fuel, and when the fuel is gone it is said to be extinguished, being without nourishment."

"In just the same way, all form by which one could predicate the existence of the saint is abandoned and uprooted like a fan palm, so that it will never grow up in future. The saint who is released from what is styled form is deep, immeasurable, hard to fathom, like the great ocean. It does not fit the case to say either that he is reborn or not reborn, both reborn and not reborn, or neither reborn nor not reborn". . . .

Master Ōbaku (Huang Po):

Gautama Buddha refuted the notion that enlightenment will lead to the perception of a universal substance composed of particles which some hold to be gross and others subtle.

How is it possible that Gautama Buddha, who denied all such views . . . could have originated the present conceptions of enlightenment? But as these doctrines are still commonly taught, people become involved in the duality of longing for "light" and eschewing "darkness." In their anxiety to *seek* enlightenment on the one hand and to *escape* from the passions and ignorance of corporeal existence on the other, they conceive of an enlightened Buddha and unenlightened sentient beings as separate entities. Continued indulgence in such dualistic concepts as these will lead to your rebirth among the six orders of beings life after life, aeon upon aeon, forever and forever! And why is it thus? Because of falsifying the doctrine that the original source of the Buddhas is that self-existent Nature. Let me assure you again that the Buddha dwells not in light, nor sentient beings in darkness, for the Truth allows no such distinctions. The Buddha is not mighty, nor sentient beings feeble, for the Truth allows no such distinctions. The Buddha is not enlightened nor sentient beings ignorant, for the Truth allows no such distinctions. It is all because you take it upon yourself to talk of *explaining* Zen!

Master Hakuin

A nobleman asked Master Hakuin: "What happens to the enlightened man at death? What happens to the unenlightened man?"

The master replied: "Why ask me?"

"Because you're a Zen master!"

"Yes," said Hakuin, "but not a dead one!"

Four: **DYING**

DYING: OF THE MASTERS

I shan't die, I shan't go anywhere,
  I'll be here;
But don't ask me anything,
  I shan't answer.
                 —Death verse of Master Ikkyū

Riding this wooden upside-down horse,
I'm about to gallop through the void.
Would you seek to trace me?
Ha! Try catching the tempest in a net.
                 —Death verse of Master Kukoku

  Dimly for thirty years;
Faintly for thirty years—
  Dimly and faintly for sixty years:
At my death I pass my feces and offer them
  to Brahmā.
                 —Written by Master Ikkyū
                   as death approached

Master Chuho (Chung-feng):

I want to die with a premonition of death a week beforehand, with my mind serenely unshaken and free from attachment to my body, thence to be reborn into the realm of the Buddhas so as to ultimately gain supreme enlightenment through them and receive their sanction, the better that I may be able to save all sentient beings throughout the innumerable worlds.

Master Fugai

When he sensed that death was near, Fugai had one of the monks dig a deep pit. Fugai then climbed into it and, standing there with immense dignity, directed the monk to cover him with earth.

Master Takkan (Ta-kuan)

Takkan was dying. His disciples asked that he write a death poem. He refused, but when they insisted, he wrote the character *Yume*, Dream, and died.

Bashō:

From olden times it has been customary to leave behind a death-poem, and perhaps I should do the same. But every moment of life is the last, every poem a death poem! Why then at this time should I write one? In these my last hours I have no poem.

Master Tennō (T'ien-huang)

When the master was dying, he called to his room the monk in charge of food and clothing in the temple. When the monk sat down by the bed, Tennō asked, "Do you understand?"

"No," the monk replied.

Tennō, picking up his pillow, hurled it through the window, and fell back dead.

Master Razan (Lo-shan)

When he sensed that death was close, Razan called everyone into the Buddha-hall and ascended the lecture seat. First he held his left hand open for several minutes. No one understood, so he told the monks from the eastern side of the monastery to leave. Then he held his right hand open. Still no one understood, so he told the monks from the western side of the monastery to leave. Only the laymen remained. He said to them: "If any of you really want to show gratitude to Buddha for his compassion to you, spare no efforts in spreading the Dharma. Now, get out! Get out of here!" Then, laughing loudly, the master fell over dead.

Master Hofuku (Pao-fu)

The master called his monks together and said, "During the last week my energy has been draining—certainly no cause for worry. It's just that death is near."

A monk asked, "You are about to die. What meaning does it have? We will continue living. And what meaning does that have?"

"They are both the Way," the master replied.

"But how can I reconcile the two?" asked the monk.

Hofuku answered, "When it rains it pours," and wrapping his legs in the full lotus, calmly died.

Rōshi Taji

As Rōshi Taji, a contemporary Zen master, approached death, his senior disciples assembled at his bedside. One of them, remembering the rōshi was fond of a certain kind of cake, had spent half a day searching the pastry shops of Tokyo for this confection, which he now presented to Rōshi Taji. With a wan smile the dying rōshi accepted a piece of the cake and slowly began munching it. As the rōshi grew weaker, his disciples leaned close and inquired whether he had any final words for them.

"Yes," the rōshi replied.

The disciples leaned forward eagerly. "Please tell us!"

"My, but this cake is delicious!" And with that he died.

Rōshi Yamamoto

Almost blind at the age of ninety-six and no longer able to teach or work about the monastery, Zen Master Yamamoto decided it was time to die, so he stopped eating. When asked by his monks why he refused his food, he replied that he had outlived his usefulness and was only a bother to everybody. They told him, "If you die now [January] when it is so cold, everybody will be uncomfortable at your funeral and you will be an even greater nuisance, so please eat!" He thereupon resumed eating, but when it became warm again he stopped, and not long after quietly toppled over and died.

Master Bassui

Just before he passed away, at the age of sixty, Bassui sat up in the lotus posture and to those gathered around him said, "Don't be misled! Look directly! What is this?" He repeated it loudly, then calmly died.

Sri Ramana Maharshi

"They say that I am dying, but I am not going away. Where could I go? I am here. . . ."

On Thursday, April 13, a doctor brought Sri Bhagavan [Maharshi] a palliative to relieve the congestion in the lungs, but he refused it. "It is not necessary, everything will come right within two days."

. . . At about sunset Sri Bhagavan told the attendants to sit him up. They knew already that every movement, every touch, was painful, but he told them not to worry about that. He sat with one of the attendants supporting his head. A doctor began to give him oxygen, but with a wave of his right hand he motioned him away.

Unexpectedly a group of devotees sitting on the veranda outside the hall began singing "Arunachala-Śiva." On hearing it, Sri Bhagavan's eyes opened and shone. He gave a brief smile of indescribable tenderness. From the outer edges of his eyes tears of bliss rolled down. One more deep breath, and no more. There was no struggle, no spasm, no other sign of death: only that the next breath did not come.

Master Tekisui

Master Tekisui heard that Master Dokuon was very sick and went to see him. Entering the sickroom, he straddled Dokuon, and nose to nose with the ashen face asked, "Well, how goes it?"

"Sick."

"Think you'll make it?"

"No."

Jumping up, Tekisui walked out.

A few years later Tekisui was himself close to death when

Master Keichu called on him. Asking the monk in charge if Tekisui was very sick, he was told that it was so. Keichu handed a box of cakes to the monk and said, "These are for your master. When you take these to him just tell him I said that he's lived long enough to die without regrets."

When the monk took the cakes in to Tekisui and delivered the message from Keichu, the master said nothing, but a gentle smile spread across his face.

Master Etsugen

Shortly before he died Etsugen called his monks together. It was December 1. "I've decided to die on the eighth of this month," he told them. "That's the day of the Buddha's enlightenment. If you have any questions left about the Teaching, you'd better ask them before then."

Because the master continued with his regular duties during the next few days, some of the monks thought he was having a little fun at their expense. Most, however, were struck with grief.

By the evening of the seventh nothing unusual had happened. Nonetheless that night Etsugen had them all assemble and taught them for the last time about the Buddha's enlightenment. He then arranged his affairs and went into his room.

At dawn he took a bath, put on his ceremonial robes, and sitting erect in the lotus posture composed this death poem:

> Shākyamuni descended the mountain.
> I went up.
> In my teaching, I guess I've always been
> something of a maverick.
> And now I'm off to hell—yo-ho!
> The inquisitiveness of men is pure folly.

Then, shutting his eyes, and still sitting, he died.

Master Yakusan (Yüeh-shan)

Yakusan's manner of death was of a piece with his life. When he was about to die, he yelled out, "The Hall's falling down! The Hall's falling down!" The monks brought various things and began to prop it up. Yakusan threw up his hands and said, "None of you understood what I meant!" and died.

Master Tōzan (Tung-shan)

When Tōzan was dying a monk said to him, "Master, your four elements are out of harmony, but is there anyone who is never ill?"

"There is," said Tōzan.

"Does this one look at you?" asked the monk.

"It is my function to look at him," answered Tōzan.

"How about when you yourself look at him?" asked the monk.

"At that moment I see no illness," replied Tōzan.

Master Kassan (Chia-shan)

When Kassan was about to die he called the chief monk and said to him, "I have preached the Way to the monks for many years. The profound meaning of Buddhism is to be known by each person himself. My illusory life is over, I am about to depart. You monks should go on just the same as when I was alive. You should not blindly make ordinary people miserable." Having said this, he immediately passed away.

Chuang-tzu

As Chuang-tzu approached death, his disciples wanted to give him a large and expensive funeral. But Chuang-tzu said, "The heavens and the earth will serve me as a coffin and a coffin shell. The sun and moon and stars will decorate my bier. All creation will be at hand to witness the event. What more need I than these?"

His disciples gasped, "We're afraid that carrion kites and crows will eat the body of our master!"

Chuang-tzu replied, "Above the ground my flesh will feed the crows and kites, below the ground, the ants and cricket-moles. Why rob one to feed the other?"

The Sixth Patriarch of Zen

On the eighth day of the seventh month the master said to his monks: "Gather around me. I have decided to leave this world . . . in the eighth month."

When Fa-hai and the other monks heard this they wept openly.

"For whom are you crying?" the master asked. "Are you worrying about me because you think I don't know where I'm going? If I didn't know, I wouldn't be able to leave you this way. What you're really crying about is that *you* don't know where I'm going. If you actually knew, you couldn't possibly cry because [you would be aware that] the True-nature is without birth or death, without going or coming. . . ."

On the day the master died he wrote a death verse and then said to the disciples, "Take good care of yourselves. I am going to leave you now. After I have left do not cry like people attached to the world. Do not accept condolences or money. Above all, do not wear mourning. It would not be in accordance with the correct Dharma and you would be no disciples of mine if you did these things. Live as though I were still here. Do zazen together. When there is calm, neither activity nor passivity, without [notions of] birth or death, coming or going, right or wrong, and without abiding or departing, then that is the great Way. When I am gone, just practice correctly according to the Teaching, just as you did during my days with you.

Remember, even were I to remain in this world, if you diso-
beyed my teaching my presence among you would be pointless."

After saying this the master became silent. Suddenly at mid-
night he entered Nirvāna. He was seventy-six.

Socrates

Crito made a sign to the servant, who was standing by; he
went out, and returned with the jailer carrying the cup of poison. Socrates said: "You, my good friend, who are experienced
in these matters shall give me directions how I am to proceed."

The man answered: "You have only to walk about until your
legs are heavy, and then to lie down, and the poison will act."

At the same time he handed the cup to Socrates, who in the
easiest and gentlest manner, without the least fear or change of
color or feature, looking at the man with all his eyes, took the
cup and said: "What do you say about making a libation out of
this cup to any god? May I, or not?"

The man answered: "We only prepare, Socrates, just so much
as we deem enough."

"I understand," he said, "but I may and must ask the gods to
prosper my journey from this to the other world—even so—and
so be it according to my prayer."

Then raising the cup to his lips, quite readily and cheerfully
he drank off the poison. And hitherto most of us had been able
to control our sorrow, but now when we saw him drinking and
saw too that he had finished the draught, we could no longer
forbear, and in spite of myself my own tears were flowing fast;
so that I covered my face and wept, not for him but at the
thought of my own calamity in having to part from such a
friend. Nor was I the first; for Crito, when he found himself
unable to restrain his tears, had got up, and I [Plato] followed;
and at that moment Apollodorus, who had been weeping all the

time, broke out in a loud and passionate cry which made cowards of us all.

Socrates alone retained his calmness: "What is this strange outcry?" he said. "I sent away the women mainly in order that they might not misbehave in this way, for I have been told that a man should die in peace. Be quiet, then, and have patience."

When we heard his words we were ashamed and refrained our tears; and he walked about until, as he said, his legs began to fail, and then he lay on his back, according to directions, and the man who gave him the poison now and then looked at his feet and legs; and after a while he pressed his foot hard and asked him if he could feel; and he said, "No"; and then his leg, and so upwards and upwards, and showed us that he was cold and stiff.

And he felt them himself, and said: "When the poison reaches the heart, that will be the end."

He was beginning to grow cold about the groin when he uncovered his face, for he had covered himself up, and said—they were his last words—he said: "Crito, I owe a cock to Asclepius; will you remember to pay the debt?"

"The debt shall be paid," said Crito. "Is there anything else?"

There was no answer to this question, but in a minute or two a movement was heard, and the attendants uncovered him. His eyes were set, and Crito closed his eyes and mouth.

Such was the end, Echecrates, of our friend, concerning whom I may truly say that of all men of his time whom I have known he was the wisest and justest and best.

The Buddha

... He then went to Kuśinagara, bathed in the river, and gave this order to Ānanda [his favorite disciple]: "Arrange a couch for me between those twin sal trees. In the course of this night the Tathāgata will enter nirvāna". ...

In full sight of his disciples he lay down on his right side, rested his head on his hand, and put one leg over the other. At that moment the birds uttered no sound, and, as if in trance, they sat with their bodies all relaxed. The winds ceased to move the leaves of the trees, and the trees shed wilted flowers, which came down like tears. . . .

They paid homage to him and then, anguish in their minds, stood around him. And the Sage spoke to them as follows: "In the hour of joy it is not proper to grieve. Your despair is quite inappropriate, and you should regain your composure. The goal, so hard to win, which for many aeons I have wished for, now at last it is no longer far away. When that is won—no earth or water, fire, wind or ether present; unchanging bliss beyond all objects of the senses, a peace which none can take away, the highest thing there is; and when you hear of that and know that no becoming mars it and nothing ever there can pass away—how is there room for grief then in your minds? At Gaya, at the time when I won enlightenment, I got rid of the causes of becoming, which are nothing but a gang of harmful vipers; now the hour comes near when I get rid also of this body, the dwelling place of the acts accumulated in the past. Now that at last this body, which harbors so much ill, is on its way out; now that at last the frightful dangers of becoming are about to be extinct; now that at last I emerge from the vast and endless suffering—is that the time for you to grieve?". . . .

And the Best of Men, aiming at their welfare and tranquility, addressed to them these meaningful words: "It is indeed a fact that salvation cannot come from the mere sight of me. It demands strenuous efforts in the practice of yoga [zazen]. But if someone has thoroughly understood this my Dharma, then he is released from the net of suffering, even though he never cast his eyes on me. A man must take medicine to be cured; the mere sight of the physician is not enough. Likewise the mere sight of me enables no one to conquer suffering; he will have to meditate for himself about the gnosis I have communicated. If self-controlled, a man may live away from me as far as can be, but if he only sees my Dharma, then indeed he sees me also. But if he should neglect to strive in concentrated calm for higher things, then though he live quite near me, he is far away from me. Therefore be energetic, persevere, and try to control your minds. Do good deeds, and try to win mindfulness!"

DYING: PRACTICAL INSTRUCTIONS

A man who dies before he dies
does not die when he dies.
                    —Abraham a Sancta Clara

One who sees the Way in the morning
can gladly die in the evening.
                    —Confucius

Abandon life and the world
that you may know the
life of the world.
                    —Rumi

Philip Kapleau:

You have asked for the teachings of the Buddha and Enlightened Ones on dying, how, when the time comes, you can pass from this state of existence to another, like a pilgrim embarking on a spiritual journey, your mind serene and unshaken by physical pain or mental anguish. You ask this not only to secure for yourselves a more felicitous rebirth but to help allay both your own fears and those of your family and close friends at the time of death. You also wish to know about meaningful funeral rites leading to a better rebirth which you may be called upon to perform in the absence of a guide with true spiritual strength. These are profoundly important questions. The answers that follow are not merely my own ideas. They have come from my masters, inspired by their masters, reaching back to the Buddha himself, each one expressing the spirit of the original teaching in the context of his own time and culture.

To the Person Approaching Death

You who are soon to relinquish this body and take another, while your mind is yet unclouded and you are relatively free of pain, hear, believe, and do what the Enlightened Ones teach about preparation for the process of dying. Do not allow doubt or cynicism to come between you and these Enlightened Ones at this critical hour. First, understand that just as you were born into this world when your karma drew you, so you are now to die at your karmic hour. You have passed through these same shadows many times, though you don't remember, and you

77

have experienced many rebirths. While you must enter the kingdom of death alone with your karma of good and evil, there is no cause for trembling. Countless Buddhas and Bodhisattvas in all realms of existence, from the deepest hells to the highest Buddha lands, wait just beyond the wall of your own ego to guide you. Open yourself to them. They have no other purpose than to release you from the sufferings of recurring birth and death.

Who and what are these great Buddhas and Bodhisattvas? They are beings who through complete enlightenment have become Perfect Ones, whole in themselves, "those in whom all spiritual and psychic faculties have come to a state of perfect harmony, and whose consciousness encompasses the infinity of the universe."[6] The essential nature of all Bodhisattvas is a great loving heart, and all living beings constitute the object of their love. Herein is the basis of the natural affinity between these Enlightened Ones and human beings, an affinity which operates on all levels. Just as a receiver tuned to a specific wavelength can pick up broadcasts thousands of miles distant, so you can receive the boundless aid of the Enlightened Ones if only you attune yourself to the vibrations of their pure minds. Do not forget that these Buddhas once were like you, and in the future you, like them, can attain the highest enlightenment if now you place complete trust in them and their teaching.

While your mind is yet clear and your energies sufficiently strong, put yourself more intensely into the presence of these Buddhas by taking the Three Refuges. Ideally you should receive them from an ordained follower of the Buddha's Way because he, having dedicated his life to the Three Treasures and thus placed himself in the orbit of the Enlightened, carries the spiritual authority to transmit the Buddha's teachings. However, if you have no such guide, raise your hands palm to palm and intone: "I take refuge in the Buddhas and pray that I may with all other beings understand the Great Way whereby the Buddha-seed in me may forever thrive. I take refuge in the Dharma [i.e., the Law, which is their teaching] and pray that I may with all beings enter deeply into this treasure whereby my wisdom may grow as vast as the ocean. I take refuge in the wisdom and warmth of the Sangha [i.e., community of those who tread this path] and pray that nothing will impede my progress toward enlightenment."

This commitment to the Three Refuges places you firmly in the lap of the Buddhas (past and present), who having confirmed the profound value of these refuges urge all beings, living and dying, to embrace them. However, simply to take refuge in these Three Treasures is not enough. To become a true child of the Buddhas you must restrain your cravings and passions—even your passion for life—and surrender your ego-self with all its demands to their compassion and mercy. You must be able to say, "Wholly and without reserve I dedicate myself to the company of the Enlightened and their spiritual sons. Take possession of me. With humility I offer myself as your servant. Having become your property I have nothing more to fear in this world. I will do only what is helpful to other beings. Through hatred and infatuation I have done many wrong things. I have not realized that I am only a traveler passing through this world. Day and night, without cessation, vitality decreases and death approaches. This very day therefore I will take my refuge in the great and powerful protectors of the world. From the bottom of my heart I take my refuge in the teaching and in the multitude of Bodhisattvas. With hands raised palm to palm I implore the Enlightened Perfect Ones in all the regions of the universe: May you kindle the light of truth for all those who on account of their delusions would otherwise fall into the abyss of misery."[7]

While your strength permits, you should also take the ten moral precepts, which are the active expression of your Buddha-mind. Embraced with sincerity, they will support and uphold you at this critical hour. Here, too, if your guide is an ordained follower of the Buddha's Way, let him give them to you. If not, you will have to do this for yourself. Do not conclude that because you will soon relinquish your body the taking of the precepts is in vain. Listen to what Zen Master Dōgen says about this: "By accepting and upholding the precepts in your deepest heart you can eventually attain to supreme enlightenment. . . . Who could possibly reject this? Buddhas have shown to countless living beings that when they wholeheartedly take into their life the moral precepts they do in time attain Buddhahood, becoming Perfectly Enlightened. . . . All the Realized Ones dwell here and embrace everything in their infinite wisdom. Those who live and have their being in this state see no distinction between themselves and others, between a subject and an object. At this time every thing—earth, plants, fence posts, bricks or pebbles, no matter what—functions as Buddha. . . . The wind and fire [i.e., inner energies] fanned by the profound influence of Buddhas [as a result of the acceptance of the precepts] drive one into the intimacy of enlightenment. This is the awakening of the wisdom mind."[8]

The Ten Precepts

I resolve not to kill but to cherish all life.

I resolve not to take what is not given but to respect the things of others.

I resolve not to engage in improper sexuality but to practice purity of mind and self-restraint.

I resolve not to lie but to speak the truth.

I resolve not to cause others to use liquors or drugs which confuse or weaken the mind, nor to do so myself, but to keep my mind clear.

I resolve not to speak of the misdeeds of others but to be understanding and sympathetic.

I resolve neither to praise myself nor to condemn others but to overcome my own shortcomings.

I resolve not to withhold spiritual or material aid but to give it freely where needed.

I resolve not to become angry but to exercise control.

I resolve not to revile the Three Treasures (i.e., the Buddha, the Dharma, and the Sangha) but to cherish and uphold them.

No matter where you are in your last hours, in so far as you can control your circumstances do not allow your mind to be weakened by drugs or other treatments which numb or impair the clarity of your consciousness. If your pain becomes too intense, let your doctor or attendant ease it with drugs which do not render you unconscious.

Your state of mind at the time you draw your last breath is crucial, for upon this hinges your following rebirth. Only a disciplined or spiritually prepared mind can hope to resist the pull of karmic forces—i.e., old patterns of craving and clinging —as the final energies are slipping away so that a higher level of rebirth, and even enlightenment itself, may be attained. The impulses of thought, feeling, and perception all gather together in this last breath with great potency.

To steady your mind and prepare yourself for the culminating moment, read, or have read to you, in measured meter, the

Heart of Perfect Wisdom.[9] Among traditional literature it has been handed down as one of the most efficacious documents for the liberation of the mind from painful bondage to birth and death. It contains the heart of the wisdom taught by all Buddhas. "Perfect Wisdom" means wisdom that goes beyond conceptual knowledge, i.e., beyond birth and death.

Heart of Perfect Wisdom

(Prajñā Pāramitā)[10]

The Bod-hi-satt-va of Com-pas-sion[11]
from the depths of praj-ñā wis-dom
saw the emp-ti-ness of all five
skan-dhas and sun-dered the bonds
that caused him suf-fer-ing.[12]

Know then:
Form here is on-ly emp-ti-ness,[13]
emp-ti-ness on-ly form.
Form is no oth-er than emp-ti-ness,
emp-ti-ness no oth-er than form.

Feel-ing, thought and choice,[14]
con-scious-ness it-self
are the same as this.

Dhar-mas here are emp-ty,
all are the pri-mal void.[15]
None take birth or die.
Nor are they stained or pure,
nor do they wax or wane.

So in emp-ti-ness no form,
no feel-ing, thought or choice,
nor is there con-scious-ness.

No eye, ear, nose,
tongue, bo-dy, mind;
no col-or, sound, smell,
taste, touch or what the mind
takes hold of,
nor e-ven act of sens-ing.

No ig-nor-ance or end of it
nor all that comes of ig-nor-ance:
no with-er-ing, no death,
no end of them.

Nor is there pain or cause of pain
or cease in pain or noble path
to lead from pain,
not e-ven wis-dom to at-tain.
At-tain-ment too is emp-ti-ness.

So know that the Bod-hi-satt-va,
hold-ing to noth-ing what-ev-er
but dwell-ing in praj-ñā wis-dom,
is freed of de-lu-sive hin-drance,
rid of the fear bred by it,
and reach-es clear-est nir-vā-na.

All Bud-dhas of past and pre-sent,
Bud-dhas of fu-ture time,
us-ing this praj-ñā wis-dom
come to full and per-fect vi-sion.

Hear then the great dhā-ra-nī,
the ra-diant, peer-less man-tra,
the Praj-ñā Pā-ra-mi-tā,
whose words al-lay all pain.
Taught by High-est Wis-dom,

true be-yond all doubt,
hear and know its truth:

Ga-te, ga-te
par-a-ga-te
par-a-sam-ga-te
bod-hi, sva-há![16]

To "prepare yourself" through the Heart of Perfect Wisdom means carefully to read and reflect upon it daily, trying to perceive its inner meaning with your intuitive consciousness. You should understand that at the time of sinking into the death coma your intellect ceases to function, and unless the truths of this sūtra have permeated the deepest strata of your consciousness they will not be available to guide you. Should you who are dying have a specific spiritual practice which you have been following, continue with it. But if you have none, then repeat the last four lines, "Ga-te, ga-te," etc., over and over as you cross the threshhold of "death." Thus you will take the sūtra with you into the intermediate state of consciousness. The reciting of these lines with a believing heart will prepare you in the best possible way for the next stage of your journey, which starts with the surrender of your normal waking consciousness.

The teachings of the Heart of Perfect Wisdom may also be taken as a guide through the intermediate, or after-death, state. All lights, visions, and apparitions of any kind which you may encounter are to be regarded as mere projections and reflexes of your own mind states and hence as empty of substance in this realm as in the dimension of waking consciousness. It was just this profound realization which brought perfect enlightenment to the Bodhisattva Avalokita, whom the Buddha refers to in the Heart of Perfect Wisdom as the "Bodhisattva of Compassion." And out of this vast compassion Avalokita (Jap., Kannon; Ch.,

Küan-yin) makes his transcendental wisdom available to all who turn to him with a sincere heart. The recitation of this Heart of Perfect Wisdom, and especially the closing four lines, is simultaneously an appeal for his concern and an opportunity for your own enlightenment.

To the One Guiding the Mind of the Dying

Yours is a vital role. It is to guide the mind of the dying both before and after death in order to awaken him to the relativity of birth and death. Always remember that the liberation of essential Mind from the confines of the body-mind through the death process offers a unique opportunity for enlightenment.

Should you undertake to guide the mind of the dying person it must only be with his clear consent. You must respect fully any indication that he wishes to be alone. However, when you do speak to him or begin to read, always address him by name so as to draw his attention.

You will be expected to read aloud from the sacred writings until the last breath is drawn. Further, you will conduct the funeral rites both at the time of death and afterward. This is tantamount to guiding the deceased in his initial steps into the after-death state.

To be effective in all this you must begin by calming the anxieties of the one you are trying to help, and this is possible only if your own mind is clear and steady and you have no reservations about the validity of these teachings. Do not attempt this role if you cannot do so wholeheartedly, since your lack of conviction would inevitably communicate itself to the dying and affect him adversely.

Needless to say, you will inform the dying of the death rites you are to perform sufficiently in advance so that he can grasp their significance and be prepared when the time of his death comes.

Create a serene atmosphere for the last hours of the dying. Arrange his room so that he has a feeling of comfortable familiarity. If the person has a favorite picture of the Buddha or other sacred figure, place it where he can easily see it. The family and friends should make their farewells brief, well before the final hour sets in. Then they should be kept out of his room so that his state of mind can be peaceful and composed, allowing him to concentrate all his attention upon these last steps.

When you observe that the dying is no longer in a position to do anything for himself, you should take over the chanting of the Heart of Perfect Wisdom in order to prevent his mind from drifting aimlessly. Put your lips close to his ear and utter each word distinctly. Keep in mind that the sense of hearing is the last to go. It is therefore of prime importance that this channel of communication between you and the dying be unobstructed by any talk irrelevant to his needs and state of mind.

After death has occurred and the body has been prepared for cremation or burial, you will have to provide a suitable funeral service, one that takes into account the wishes of the family as well as those of the deceased. A temporary altar should be erected in the room where the service is to be held and a picture of the departed placed upon it. If possible, a figure of a Buddha or Bodhisattva should also be placed on the altar together with suitable offerings, such as flowers, incense, food, and lighted candles. The photograph acts as a focus to direct the minds and feelings of those present to the consciousness of the deceased, while the offerings to the Buddha (which include silent prayer) establish a link between Buddhas and the departed, between Buddhas and the living, and between the living and the departed.

You may begin the service with a tribute to the one who has

died, after which recite the following prayer reverently, one phrase at a time, with all those present repeating after you. The entire prayer is best recited three times. The sincere recitation of this prayer will help invoke Bodhisattvic forces for the benefit of the deceased.

The Prayer

O Buddhas and Bodhisattvas, abiding in all directions, endowed with great compassion, endowed with fore-knowledge, endowed with the divine eye, endowed with love, affording protection to sentient beings, condescend through the power of your great compassion to come forth; condescend to accept these offerings concretely laid out and mentally created.

O Compassionate Ones, you who possess the wisdom of understanding, the love of compassion, the power of doing divine deeds and of protecting in incomprehensible measure: [such-and-such person] is passing from this world to the next. He is taking a great leap. The light of this world has faded for him. He has entered solitude with his karmic forces. He has gone into a vast Silence. He is borne away by the Great Ocean [of birth and death].

O Compassionate Ones, protect [so-and-so], who is defenseless. Be to him like a father and a mother.

O Compassionate Ones, let not the force of your compassion be weak, but aid him. Let him not go into miserable states of existence. Forget not your ancient vows . . .[17]

The service may be concluded with the chanting of the Heart of Perfect Wisdom by all present, followed by the Four Vows of a Bodhisattva, also recited three times in succession:

I resolve to become enlightened for the
sake of all living beings.

I will cut the roots of all delusive passions.

I will penetrate the farthest gate of Dharma.

I will realize the Supreme Way of Buddha.

The funeral service concluded, it will be your further duty to recite daily for the next seven days the Heart of Perfect Wisdom and the Prayer. Three times in succession the sūtra should be chanted clearly toward the picture of the deceased in a continuing effort to bring him to enlightenment. Food, flowers and candles should be offered anew during this interval for the same reasons stated previously. Incense also should be offered to the Buddhas and Bodhisattvas at every service. These rites are to be repeated once a week on the day of death for the following six weeks, or forty-nine days in all. Performed in harmony with the seven-day birth-and-death cycle in the intermediate state,[18] they have as their purpose the awakening of the Mind of the deceased before he enters his next realm of existence. Because the time of rebirth is variable, the rites are extended into yearly cycles.

These forty-nine-day post-mortem rites are every bit as valid even where death comes through sudden accident, allowing no time for the preparation of the mind of the victim, or where death overtakes him in a remote or inaccessible location so that his body or cremated remains are not present at the funeral. Here a photograph of the deceased is of special significance.

This completes your formal duties. You can now see that when these rites have been performed in a selfless and sincere way their value to the deceased is inestimable. Moreover, you yourself by virtue of having transmitted these teachings to someone in extreme need have sown the seeds of a karma which will benefit both yourself and the deceased immeasurably.

To the Family

When it is certain that a member of the family does not have long to live, a spiritual guide or adviser should be selected to prepare him for "death" and to arrange for the funeral and postfuneral rites. If he belongs to a church or temple, his clergyman should be summoned. If, however, he has no such formal affiliation, a friend of spiritual maturity should be chosen—if possible with his consent—to act in the capacity of spiritual guide, using the teachings and instructions contained in this book. A member of the family could just as well assume this role provided he were confident of his composure throughout the rites.

Especially in his last hours should you give the dying your warm support, for each and every member of the family has a karmic bond with him. Listen carefully to whatever he may say, neither arguing with nor contradicting him. If he rails against God or his doctor or anyone else, let him do so, though this reaction is unlikely if he has read and reflected upon the foregoing teachings. Do not force him to discuss such practical matters as the making of a will if his mind does not move in that direction. For any member of the family to impose his own wishes in these last hours, when the dying person needs complete peace to concentrate his dwindling energy for his passage through "death," would be karmically harmful to all involved.

The family should also be aware that those approaching death may reach a point where they lose interest in their surroundings and withdraw from those around them into a trancelike state, often seeing or hearing things which others are not experiencing. The family should not interpret this as evidence of the deterioration of the mind or memory of the dying, assuming that he can now be safely ignored. In fact his hearing and understanding may be even more acute. Many ancient traditions say that individuals often develop extrasensory perception during severe or terminal illness. It can thus be seen that any excessive weeping or hysteria will almost certainly disturb these sensitive processes going on within the dying; therefore keep these demonstrations as far from the deathbed as possible.

After the attending physician makes the pronouncement of death and issues a death certificate, an undertaker will have to attend to the body. Various writings on the art of dying say that, where possible, three days should elapse before the body is embalmed, cut up or treated in any way so as to permit the life-forces to withdraw from the body and enter the intermediate stage.[19] If necessary, this can be accomplished by asking the undertaker to seal the remains in a metal-lined box or casket for the three-day period. When the three days have passed, the body is then cremated or buried.

It cannot be stressed too often that the funeral rites are for the benefit of the deceased himself, and that the family must comply with his expressed wishes as to who shall perform them, and how. Similarly, his instructions for the disposition of his own body and the performance of subsequent rites must not be ignored. If ostentatious funeral trappings have no meaning for him, to indulge in them in his presumed honor would serve neither him nor his family, whose true role should be to insure in every way possible a serene death and pain-free rebirth for him.

The family would do well to participate in both the death rites and the postfuneral ceremonies which take place in the forty-nine-day interval. In thus reaffirming their karmic link with the deceased they will ease their loneliness and constructively channel their grief. Beyond this level, however, and in an ultimate sense grief itself is without substance, for as the Heart of Perfect Wisdom states, "no withering, no death. . . . Nor is there pain or cause of pain. . . ." The Mind of the "dead" and the Mind of the "living" are intrinsically One. This One can in no way be diminished. Not even the dead can disappear. Where, after all, would they go?

NOTES

1. Karlis Osis, "Deathbed Observations by Physicians and Nurses," *Journal of the American Society for Psychical Research* (October 1963).

2. A reference to a story in the Angulimāla Sūtra in which a revengeful teacher tells his innocent disciple he will be reborn in the Pure Land (q.v.) if he will kill a thousand men. The disciple, needing one more murder to fulfill his bloody mission, pursues the Buddha, who not only foils his diabolical purpose but brings about in him a change of heart.

3. Tenko-San, *A New Road to Ancient Truth* (London: George Allen & Unwin,) quoted by Marie Byles in *World Buddhism, Vesak Annual* (2514-1970), p. 83.

4. Vijnàptimatràsiddhi-Sàstra.

5. Momentary birth and death in the intermediate state parallels the constant creation and destruction going on within the cells of the material body. The meaning of "ordinary birth and death" in the intermediate state is that normally at the end of every seven days the "entity," if it has not yet reincarnated, dies and continues to be reborn in the same intermediate state. This death corresponds to the death of the material body in the normal waking state at the end of a lifetime.

6. Lama Govinda, *Foundations of Tibetan Mysticism* (New York: E. P. Dutton & Co., 1960), p. 41.

7. Sàntideva, *Bodhicaryàvatàra, Part II,* quoted in *Foundations of Tibetan Mysticism.*

8. Zen Master Dōgen, *Shōbōgenzō,* quoted by Reihō Masunaga in *Zen for Daily Living* (Shunjūsha Pub. Co., Tokyo, 1964).

9. In this sūtra the Buddha is speaking to Sāriputra, wisest among his disciples, about the achievement of Avalokita, who became the Bod-

hisattva of Compassion through his discovery that the human personality is made up of five skandhas (q.v.) and that they are empty
of enduring substance. The hyphenation is for purposes of chanting.
10. Prajñā Pāramitā: wisdom that "goes beyond," i.e., transcendental
wisdom; it is also the path leading to the attainment of this wisdom,
and the text containing the teaching conducive to its realization.
11. Bodhisattva of Compassion: Avalokita or Avalokiteśvara in Sanskrit;
Kanzeon or Kannon in Japanese; Küan-yin in Chinese. He is often
depicted with many arms, representing his endless "helping hands,"
and with many heads, signifying his various kinds of wisdom.
12. Five skandhas: lit., "heaps" or "aggregates" (i.e., form, feeling,
perception, mental tendencies or impulses, consciousness).
13. "Here": i.e., on the level of transcendental wisdom.
14. "Thought": lit., "perceptions." "Choice": included in this blanket
term are mental dispositions, tendencies, impulses, volitions, etc.
15. Dharma—dharmas: with a small d, plural, the fundamental elements of existence, tangible and intangible. Force, substance, form,
cause and effect are produced by the play of these dharmas, which
are essentially neutral. Dharma with a capital D and no s: universal
Law, Truth, Buddhist doctrine, teachings of the Buddha.
16. Since the correct pronunciation of these Sanskrit lines increases
their effectiveness, they are here set out phonetically:

> Gə-tay, gə-tay
> pah-rah gə-tay
> pah-rah som-gə-tay
> bod-hi sva-há!

These lines can be rendered into English as:

> Gone, gone
> gone beyond,
> fully beyond,
> Awake: rejoice!

The word "sva-há," accented on the second syllable, has no exact
English equivalent. It is a word of exultation, like "hallelujah."
17. Adapted from *The Tibetan Book of the Dead*, W. Y. Evans-Wentz,
ed. (London: Oxford University Press, 1965).
18. See article by Rōshi Yasutani, pp. 41–44.

19. In practice, however, the time has varied from one to three days, depending on climate and other factors. And of course in some instances, as when the deceased has donated his organs or body to a hospital or medical school, a wait of even one day would be impossible.

GLOSSARY

Words marked Skt. *are Sanskrit; those with* J., *Japanese; and those with* Ch. *are Chinese. Technical words and expressions not defined in the text are explained in the Glossary.*

Amitābha (*J.*, Amida): the Buddha of infinite life and light; the central figure in the Pure Land Sect of Buddhism.

Arunachala-Śiva: a hymn. Arunachala is the sacred mountain near which Ramana Maharshi spent his adult life. Śiva, Brahmā and Vishṇu constitute the Hindu Triad. Śiva represents destruction, but also sustains and offers grace to the suffering world.

bhikshu: the Sanskrit term for an ordained follower of the Buddha's Way; a monk.

birth and death: relativity; time and space; cause and effect; karma; samsāra; endless change.

Bodhisattva (lit., "wisdom-being"): in Buddhism, an extraordinary being of great compassion whose spiritual development is just below that of a Buddha; also one who vows to strive for enlightenment for the sake of all sentient beings.

Brahmā: the Supreme God of post-Vedic Hinduism; Absolute Reality.

Buddha: a Sanskrit word meaning (1) ultimate Truth or absolute Mind, and (2) one fully awakened to the true nature of existence. *The* Buddha refers to the historical Siddhartha Gotama, also called the Tathāgata (q.v.). Buddhism teaches that he was one of a long line of Buddhas, each the Teacher of humanity in his own world cycle, and will be succeeded by other Buddhas in subsequent epochs.

Buddha-nature: the substratum of Wholeness intrinsic to both sentient and insentient life.

ego: in Buddhism, the delusional notion of one's self as a discrete, separated entity.

97

eight falsities: false views concerning creation, destruction, past, future, the one, the many, change, and permanence.

Enlightened Ones: fully perfected Buddhas and Bodhisattvas.

five lusts: the attachment to (1) wealth, (2) sex, (3) food and drink, (4) fame, and (5) sleep.

four sins of the mouth: (1) lying, (2) using immoral language, (3) gossiping, (4) slandering.

Gautama (Pāli, Gotama): the surname of Shākyamuni Buddha.

Gaya: a town in northeastern India where the Buddha came to Great Enlightenment under the Bo tree.

guru: a spiritual teacher or guide.

Hīnayāna (i.e., the "Smaller Vehicle"; see "Mahāyāna"): the Buddhism of Southeast Asia.

illusion: in Buddhism, the misinterpretation of objective reality; delusion, a belief in something contrary to reality.

Judge of the Dead: in Buddhist mythology, Yama-rāja, who holds up the Mirror of Knowledge (q.v.) to the dead.

Kamma: (Pāli) meaning karma.

kōan: a nonlogically formulated spiritual problem which is often used in Zen teaching; there are about seventeen hundred recorded kōans.

Kuśinagara: a town in northeastern India where the Buddha passed from this existence, or entered parinirvāna.

Mahāyāna (i.e., the "Larger Vehicle"; see "Hīnayāna"): the Buddhism of Japan, Tibet, China, Korea, and other north Asian countries.

mantra: sacred sounds recited in tantric Buddhist and Hindu sects as a means to spiritual awakening.

māyā: illusion, or reality as it is ordinarily perceived under the veil of illusion.

Middle Path: the Middle Way, i.e., the Buddha's Dharma, or Teaching.

Mind: absolute Reality; total Awareness; with a small m: the seat of the intellect.

Mirror of Knowledge (Mirror of Karma): in Buddhist mythology, the mirror in which the "dead" see reflected all their past karma.

Mumonkan: a collection of 48 kōans compiled by Zen Master Mumon (Ch., Wu-mēn Hui-k'ai) in about the year 1228.

nirvāna: the final state into which beings enter when they are no longer bound by the consciousness of an illusory ego.

Pure Land (J., Jōdo): the world of Truth and Purity.

rōshi: venerable (spiritual) teacher or master.

samādhi: in Buddhism, intense yet effortless concentration; absorption to the point of self-forgetfulness.

satori: enlightenment or Self-realization.

self-Self: with a lower case *s*, the limited ego-entity, the "I" whose boundaries are the senses and the discriminating intellect; with an upper case *S*, the selfless, boundless "I."

Shōbōgenzō (lit., *A Treasury of the Eye of the True Dharma*): Zen Master Dōgen's magnum opus, consisting of 95 sections, written over a period of 25 years; completed in about 1252.

six orders of beings: beings whose karma has brought them to one of the six realms (q.v.) of unenlightened existence.

six organs of sense: eye, ear, nose, tongue, body (touch), and mind (the discriminating intellect).

six realms of existence: in Buddhist cosmology, realms of hell, hungry ghosts, beasts, fighting demons, human beings, devas. In these six unenlightened states beings are subject to unremitting birth and death according to causes and conditions.

sūtras: the Buddhist scriptures, that is, the purported dialogues and sermons of Shākyamuni Buddha.

Tathāgata (lit., "the One Thus Come," or "thus enlightened I come"): the appellation by which the Buddha referred to himself.

ten evils: (1) killing, (2) stealing, (3) committing adultery, (4) lying, (5) using immoral language, (6) gossiping, (7) slandering, (8) coveting, (9) giving vent to anger, (10) holding wrong views.

ten powers of a Buddha: complete knowledge of (1) every kind of causality; (2) the individual karma of all sentient beings; (3) all the stages of zazen leading to liberation; the various degrees of samadhi; (4) the powers and faculties of all beings; (5) the desires of all sentient beings; (6) the differing natures of sentient beings; (7) the end toward which everything moves; (8) the future lives of all sentient beings; (9) the past lives of all sentient beings; (10) how to end illusion and attain nirvāna.

Theravāda (lit., "Wisdom of the Elders"): see "Hīnayāna."

Thread of Life: karma; self-conscious or relative existence.

Three Lower States: in Buddhist cosmology, subhuman states or realms, i.e., hellish states, ghostly states, beastlike states.

three poisons: greed, anger, and delusion.

three sins of the body: (1) killing, (2) stealing, (3) committing adultery.

three stages to nirvāna (of a Bodhisattva): (1) elementary devotional practices; (2) initial desire for enlightenment followed by the vow to attain it; (3) four courses of correct behavior or conduct, including the practice of ten perfections: giving, moral purity, patience, zealousness, meditation, wisdom, adaptability, resolution, force of purpose, and knowledge.

void (*Skt.*, śūnyatā; *J.*, kū): the viable matrix of all existence: living, dynamic, devoid of mass, beyond individuality or personality.

zazen: a concentrated, one-pointed mind; the process of emptying the mind of all thought-forms, images, concepts, etc.

Zen: short for *zenna*, a Japanese transliteration of the Chinese word *Ch'anna (Ch'an)*, which is in turn a transliteration of the Sanskrit term *dhyāna* (see "zazen"), meaning a concentrated, one-pointed, stabilized mind. As a Buddhist sect, Zen's methods and disciplines emphasize the direct attainment of satori, or enlightenment, which is the heart of the Buddha's teaching.

Contributors

In the case of Chinese Ch'an (Zen) masters, the Japanese transliterations of their names appear first, followed by their Chinese names, when the material from each master comes from Japanese sources. Words marked Ch. are Chinese, those with J., Japanese.

Abraham a Sancta Clara (1644–1709): an Austrian Augustinian monk, Hans Ulrich Megerle, prolific author of theological and satirical writings.

Apollonius of Tyana: a wandering Greek seer and philosopher of the first century A.D.

Bashō (1644–1694): Japan's best-known haiku poet.

Bassui Tokusho (1327–1387): a Japanese Rinzai Zen master.

Blofeld, John: a contemporary English translator of Chinese Buddhist texts *(The Zen Teaching of Huang Po, The Zen Teaching of Hui Hai)*, and author of *The Tantric Mysticism of Tibet*.

Buddha (Siddhārtha Gautama, later known as Shākyamuni—i.e., "the silent sage of the Shākya clan"—fifth century B.C.): the towering spiritual figure upon whose teaching Buddhism was founded. For further description of the Buddha, see Glossary.

Burns, Douglas: a contemporary scholar of Theravāda Buddhism.

Chuang-tzu: the Chinese Taoist sage of the fourth century B.C. who expounded the doctrines of Lao-tzu with wit and originality.

Chuho Myohon (*Ch.*, Chung-feng Ming-pen, 1263–1323): a Chinese Ch'an (Zen) master.

Confucius (*Ch.*, Kung Fu-tsu; *J.*, Koshi; 551–479 B.C.): the renowned Chinese sage. The *Analects* is his most noted writing.

Coomaraswamy, Ananda (1877–1947): author of *Buddha and the Gospel of Buddhism* and other books on Hinduism and Indian art.

Dōgen Kigen (1200–1253): the Japanese Zen master credited with founding the Sōtō sect; probably the most seminal mind in Japanese Buddhism.

Dōgo Enchi (*Ch.*, Tao-wu Yüan-chih, 769–835): a Chinese Ch'an (Zen) master.

Dokuon (1819–1895): a Japanese Zen master.

Epictetus (50?–135?): the Greek Stoic philosopher.

Etsugen (1616–1681): a Japanese Zen master.

Fugai (1779–1847): a Japanese Zen master.

Govinda, Lama: a contemporary German-born Buddhist monk-scholar, author of *Foundations of Tibetan Mysticism, The Way of the White Clouds,* and other writings.

Hakuin Ekaku (1686–1769): the Japanese Zen master who revitalized the Rinzai Zen teaching; accomplished painter, writer, and sculptor.

Hofuku Juten (*Ch.*, Pao-fu Ts-ung-chan, ?–928): a Chinese Ch'an (Zen) master.

Ikkyū Sōjun (1394–1481): a Japanese Zen master.

Kapleau, Philip: director of the Zen Center of Rochester, New York; author of *The Three Pillars of Zen* and other writings.

Kassan (*Ch.*, Chia-shan): a Chinese Ch'an (Zen) master; his dates are unknown.

Keizan Jōkin (1268–1325): the Fourth Patriarch of the Japanese Sōtō sect of Zen after Dōgen; author of the Zen writing *Zazen Yojinki (Precautions to Observe in Zazen).*

Kukoku (1328–1407): a Japanese Zen master.

Lao-tzu (604–?): the legendary Chinese sage and author of the *Tao Teh Ching (The Way and Its Power).*

Lessing, Gotthold Ephraim (1729–81): German dramatist and philosopher.

Maharshi, Sri Ramana (1879–1950): considered to be one of modern India's deeply enlightened sages.

Matsunaga, Teitoku (1571–1653): a Japanese poet.

Milarepa, Jetsun (1052–?): "the cotton-clad one"; Tibet's great poet-sage.

Milinda (Menander, 125–95 B.C.): a Greek King of Bactria.

Nāgasena: a first-century B.C. Buddhist monk who converted King Milinda to the Buddha's Way.

Nārada, Mahāthera: a Ceylonese monk-scholar who has written and lectured extensively on Theravāda Buddhism.

Ōbaku Kiun (Ch., Huang Po Hsi-yün, ?–850): one of the great Chinese Ch'an (Zen) masters of the T'ang era.

Ramakrishna, Sri (1836-86): the Indian sage and mystic upon whose teachings the Ramakrishna (Vedanta) Order is founded.

Razan (Ch., Lo-shan): a Chinese Ch'an (Zen) master whose dates are unknown.

Rumi, Jalal ed-Din (1207–1273): a Persian Sufi poet and mystic.

Sangharakshita, Bhikshu: a contemporary English-born Mahāyāna Buddhist monk-scholar, author of The Three Jewels, A Survey of Buddhism, and other writings.

Seneca (4 B.C.–65 A.D.): the Roman statesman, writer and Stoic philosopher.

Shinran (1173–1262): the guiding light of the Jōdo Shinshu (the True Pure Land Sect) of Japanese Buddhism.

Shōzan (Ch., Shao-shan): a ninth-century Chinese Ch'an (Zen) master.

Sixth Patriarch of Zen (Ch., Hui-nēng; J., Rokuso-daishi; 638–713): the Platform Sūtra deals with his life and teaching.

Socrates (470?–399 B.C.): the Greek philosopher of Athens.

Story, Francis: a contemporary English Buddhist scholar, with long residence in Southeast Asia, who has written much on Theravāda Buddhism.

Taji, Rōshi Genki (1889–1953): a Japanese Zen master.

Takkan (Ch., Ta-kuan; 1573–1645): a Chinese Ch'an (Zen) master.

Tekisui (1822–1899): a Japanese Zen master.

Tennō Dōgo (Ch., T'ien-huang Tao-wu; 748–807): a Chinese Ch'an (Zen) master.

Tōzan Ryōkai (Ch., Tung-shan Liang-chieh; 807–869): the Chinese Ch'an (Zen) master who founded the Tsao Tung (Sōtō) sect of Zen Buddhism.

Vivekananda, Swami (1863–1902): the most distinguished disciple of Sri Ramakrishna; founder of the Ramakrishna (Vedanta) Order in America.

Voltaire, François M. A. (1694–1778): French philosopher noted for his advocacy of freedom of conscience.

Yakusan Igen (*Ch.*, Yüeh-shan Wei-yen, 751–834): a Chinese Ch'an (Zen) master.

Yamamoto, Rōshi Gempo (1865–1961): a twentieth-century Japanese Zen master.

Yasutani, Rōshi Hakuun: a contemporary Japanese Zen master; one of the teachers of Philip Kapleau.

INDEX

Numerals in italics refer to pages where terms are defined. In the case of names, numerals in italics refer to pages containing biographical information.

74 75 10 9 8 7 6 5 4 3 2 1